MANY
MANSIONS

MANY MANSIONS

by

AIR CHIEF MARSHAL
LORD DOWDING

Author of *Lychgate, The Dark Star, God's Magic*

www.whitecrowbooks.com

Many Mansions

First published November 1943
Original Copyright © 1943 by Hugh Caswall Tremenheere Dowding.
This Copyright © 2013 by David Whiting. All rights reserved.

Published and printed in the United States of America and the United Kingdom
by White Crow Books; an imprint of White Crow Productions Ltd.

For information, contact White Crow Books
at 3 Merrow Grange, Guildford, GU1 2QW United Kingdom,
or e-mail to info@whitecrowbooks.com.

Cover Designed by Butterflyeffect
Interior design by Velin@Perseus-Design.com

Paperback ISBN 978-1-910121-07-8
eBook   ISBN 978-1-910121-08-5

Non Fiction / Body, Mind & Spirit / Death & Dying

www.whitecrowbooks.com

CONTENTS

TO THE KIND FRIENDS WHO HAVE HELPED ME
WITH CRITICISM, ADVICE AND MATERIAL
THIS BOOK IS DEDICATED

CHAPTER 1

PRELIMINARY

This book is written for ordinary men by an ordinary man. It deals principally with matters which are not evident to ordinary consciousness, but I have tried very hard to keep it on the lines of ordinary commonsense, and to present my material in a manner which will be acceptable to the working—or business—man without calling upon him to do violence to his intelligence by accepting improbable and impractical theories unsupported by reasonable evidence. In a word, I shall not ask him to have Faith, in the sense of the schoolboy's definition, "Faith is the power of believing what you know to be untrue." For this reason too I shall try as far as possible to use simple words. If, for instance, I mean that a man is dead, I shall say that he is dead; not that he has "Passed the Veil" or "Moved into the Great Beyond." It will be quite obvious that I do not intend thereby to imply that bodily death is the end of all things.

In the same way I shall try, so far as may be possible, to avoid the use of technical expressions such as "Astral Body" or "Sphere of Contemplation"; but one must use some words to describe conditions not known on earth. All that I can say is that, when I have to use such expressions, I will try to define my terms.

I address myself to women as well as to men, but to men particularly through their powers of logic and reasoning. Women are swayed more than men by emotion, and are willing to take short cuts by intuition, which are rejected by the more judicially minded male. But if I can convince men, I shall convince women too.

Only they will perhaps wonder why I am making such a fuss to convince my readers of the reasonableness of things which ought to be quite self-evident.

Well now, what is the situation in the world today? Millions of people want to know what will happen to them after they die.

(It would not be an exaggeration to say that everyone wants to know this, except for the fact that a good many either know the answer already or think that they know it.) What sources are open to the ordinary man to help him towards this knowledge? Broadly speaking I should say that there are five:

(a) The Church; including the writings of philosophers who claim Divine inspiration, and whose claims are admitted by Church authorities.

(b) Non-Christian religions; including the writings of philosophers who claim Divine inspiration in accordance with their own creeds.

(c) The Spiritualists; including the writings of philosophers who claim inspiration (Divine or at a lower level) not at present acknowledged by existing creeds.

(d) The apparently uninspired workings of a man's own brain; including the writings of philosophers who do not claim external inspiration.

(e) Inspired personal communications, received either direct or through a channel which a man believes to be reliable.

I don't maintain that this is a particularly good, tidy or complete classification, or that some categories do not overlap into others; but it will serve my purpose by dividing the subject into convenient partitions for subsequent discussion.

This may be a good place to pause, to say something about myself—just enough to enable you to visualise the person who is writing to you, and to give you an idea of his qualifications, or lack of qualifications, for the task.

After an entirely undistinguished career at Winchester and "The Shop" (Royal Military Academy, Woolwich) I was commissioned in the Artillery in 1900. I served abroad, mainly in the Mountain Artillery in India, until I entered the Camberley Staff College at the end of 1911. Here I got my civil pilot's "ticket" in my spare time, and I went to the Central Flying School in January 1914. I served throughout the last war in the Royal Flying Corps and the Royal Air Force, and remained in the Air Force until my retirement. From 1930 to 1936 I was at the head of the Technical Department at the Air Ministry, and my last active appointment was as Commander-in-Chief of the Fighter Command, a post which I held until November 1940.

I have led a busy and active life, without much inclination or leisure for profound reading or philosophical study. In short, I think I may fairly claim to be the embodiment of the "Plain Blunt Man" whom my friend Mr. Arnold Lunn sets up as his imaginary opponent in his delightful works on Skiing. (Skiing, by the way, is also my own besetting intemperance.)

So far as I am aware I am completely non-psychic. I have never had any super-normal experience, and I have never attended a spiritualistic séance.* I regard this lack of personal psychic experience as an asset for my present purpose, because it ensures that the impressions on which I have formed my opinions must necessarily have been quite objective, and you will not be able to say that I ask you to accept any conclusions on evidence which is intimately personal to myself and therefore cannot be adequately communicated to you.

Well, that's enough about myself. I don't quite know how this book is going to work itself out, but I don't expect I shall have to obtrude myself on you any more.

Returning now to my Categories:

(a) For several reasons the Church is not helpful to laymen in forming their opinions on the subject of individual survival. The Church anchored its ship sixteen hundred years ago, and the capstan has rusted up. It shirks the issue, and will not openly examine and pronounce upon the mass of evidence which now exists on the subject of the future life. I shall have more to say about the Church in the next chapter.

(b) On the subject of non-Christian creeds, and their ideas on the future life, volumes might be written, but this is not going to be one of them. I have neither the qualifications nor the space to deal with such a vast question. I mention the subject principally to point out that there are large sections of the human race who

---

* This statement was literally true at the time when this book was finished (January 1943). Since then, however, I have made several friends who have received from "the other side" messages addressed to me

exhibit no curiosity about the future life because they have been supplied with a satisfactory explanation by their religion. As this book unfolds it will be seen that the tenor of the messages to which I shall draw attention is that all religions will ultimately come together at the top. That there is no cataclysmic revelation, religious or other, at the time of death, but, as the spirits of men progress after death, the false or unhelpful items of their beliefs will be almost imperceptibly shed one by one, and members of the Church of England will not be exempted from the shedding process.

(c) As this book is mainly about Spiritualism (in its widest sense) I may reasonably be asked to define what I mean by a spiritualist.

As I use the term, I mean a person who believes in the existence of discarnate spirits, and in their power of manifesting themselves to human beings by means of apparitions, physical phenomena or intelligible communications. This excludes communication already accepted into the canons of existing religions. Moses, Buddha and St. John were powerful mediums, but I do not class people as spiritualists because they believe in the validity of their messages.

I also exclude those whose beliefs are limited to phenomena such as hypnotism and telepathy and other communications between the minds of people still living on earth.

Spiritualistic messages are of great variety and diversity. They have brought comfort to thousands upon thousands of the bereaved; yet many of them give evidence of triviality and incompleteness, a fact which has deterred many thoughtful men from accepting their genuineness and from pursuing a study of the phenomena. This difficulty is perhaps susceptible of a rational explanation and I shall deal with it later.

A certain proportion of messages are definitely misleading and harmful. These generally arise from efforts to establish communication from motives of mere curiosity and with the hope of material advantage (ought I to sell Imperial Tobaccos?). With these I may class the messages and phenomena emanating from dishonest mediums.

There remain a number of messages, some of great interest and beauty, which, provided that they are true, must be of inestimable value to the human race. It is quite incomprehensible to me that these messages should have produced so little effect, and that, after creating a small ripple of interest among the general public, they should have relapsed into obscurity. Perhaps it is because spiritualism in general is discredited with the average man on account of the defects of some of its particular phenomena as indicated above; any flicker of interest aroused is soon extinguished, and the man slides back into his comfortable Materialism, with the result that the nations of the world are now mutually engaged in blowing one another to pieces.

It will be my endeavour to bring to notice these messages (or such of them as I know of) and try to present them in such a way as to enable an intelligent man to accept or reject them on their merits.

(d) I shall not say much about conclusions or doctrines which are based on no data but only on abstract thought. I do not say that such conclusions cannot be formed, because they undoubtedly can.

What I do say is that there is not much point in trying to attack them, because no ground for rational argument exists. The scientist starts by accumulating data and then develops a Hypothesis (things may be so); as the result of further work and observation, the Hypothesis becomes a Theory (things are probably so); and, in the final stage, after being checked and crosschecked, the Theory becomes a Law (things must be so). There is no arguing with a man who evolves his philosophy out of his inner consciousness.

Hitler's generals had to take second place to Hitler's Intuition.

(e) In the same way there is not much to be said by way of argument about conviction based on personal revelation. If I see a vision, or receive a message from my dead mother which bears convincing evidence of authenticity, I shall believe in her survival, and not all the argument in the world will shake me. I may be told that I have produced the whole episode from my own sub consciousness, or that my mother during life had impressed her personality on some medium which has subsequently manifested itself to me. I shall regard the explanation as being more far-fetched than what I regard as the reality. I may be right or I may be wrong, but I shall have that personal conviction which transcends all argument.

CHAPTER 2

THE CHURCH

I have said that the church is not helpful to laymen in forming their opinions on the subject of individual survival. I may be asked what I mean by "the Church," and this is a fair question in view of the great diversity of beliefs among those who profess and call themselves Christians.

I am thinking, of course, mainly about the Church of England, because it is our national Church in which I was brought up, and I know more about it than about others: but I include in my definition those other varieties of Christians who pin their faith to the Creeds as crystallised in the fourth century, and to the literal accuracy of the Epistles and Gospels of the New Testament.

A Catholic friend has asked me to point out that the Roman Church does not come under this definition, since it claims to be guided by progression and continuous revelation. I certainly had no intention of implying that the Roman Church gave no help to the layman on the subject of individual survival: that would be absurd in face of its Canonisation of Saints and prayers for the dead.

The Dominican priest, the R. Pere Mainage, professor of the History of Religions at the *Institut Catholique* in France, has for some years devoted himself officially to the study of psychic sciences.

Presumably, therefore, he is competent to define the attitude of the Catholic Church. This is what he says to Paul Heuze, an inquiring French journalist: "What does the Church think of the Spiritistic theories? That is very easy to answer, it condemns them explicitly and absolutely.

In the first place the Church has at all times forbidden the spontaneous intercourse of the living with beings beyond the tomb. . . .

Let me sum up in these few words: Spiritistic research is formally prohibited by the Church. Scientific research is not prohibited, but it is earnestly desired that this work should be left to those qualified to undertake it." (*Do the Dead Live?* By Paul Heuze.) For some profound but inscrutable reason Christ apparently took no steps to ensure that the story of His life should be recorded in writing, nor even that a contemporaneous written record should be made of His teaching. For a hundred years after His death the records depend on a chain of verbal communications starting from His unlettered Apostles, who were patently unable to understand His parables and His teaching even during the period of His ministry. The result of this was that Christianity soon split up into a great number of Sects whose practices and beliefs increasingly diverged, until almost no common factor remained except that Christ had existed and preached a Gospel of unselfishness and love.

Various Church councils were therefore held, among which that at Nicea in A.D. 335 was perhaps the most important, and at these councils the Christian faith was enclosed in a rigid orthodox framework—a framework which has remained substantially unaltered to this day.

Now, however necessary that framework was at the time of its construction, it contains certain items which are repugnant to the mentality of the modern educated man. I take 'The Resurrection of the Body' as a case in point. The early Christians were absolutely convinced, at any given time, that the second coming of Christ was imminent. They found it, therefore, a tenable theory that the bodies of the dead should lie quiescent for a few years to await that event, just as the body of Christ had lain for three days in the tomb.

But if the Resurrection is to be in the physical body, and is to be delayed for thousands of years, problems arise which are apparently insoluble. For instance, the processes of nature over a long period, or the practice of Cannibalism over a short period, might result in there being several claimants for the same body.

If you ask an Anglican clergyman about this he will probably say: "Oh, nobody believes that now"; but it remains an article of our Creed, "which except a man believe faithfully he cannot be saved." And if you ask him what teaching the Church offers as to what happens to the Soul or Spirit after death, he will probably be quite at a loss.

The fact is that the Church simply won't face the issue. It is a matter of common knowledge that a committee was appointed in 1937 by

Dr. Lang, then Archbishop of Canterbury. Its chairman was Dr. Francis Underhill, Bishop of Bath and Wells, who died in January 1943. Its terms of reference were substantially "to investigate the subject of communications with discarnate spirits, and the claims of Spiritualism in relation to Christian faith." The committee laboured for over two years; they sat with mediums and heard evidence on both sides. Finally they produced a report signed by the chairman and six others of the most prominent members of the committee. A minority report was signed by three members. The report was printed and circulated to the diocesan bishops, but Dr. Lang refused to publish it in spite of strong pressure from several quarters.

Those who are interested can obtain a pamphlet entitled *The Silence of Dr. Lang* from the Psychic Press Ltd., 144, High Holborn, W.C.1. It makes interesting reading and gives the names of the seven signatories of the main report, including a Dean, two Canons, a celebrated psychologist and a K.C. Of course I am not in a position to guarantee the accuracy of the contents of the pamphlet, but it is very circumstantial and, if it is not accurate, perhaps the best reply would be to publish the report.

It may be that the new Archbishop of Canterbury will reconsider the question of publication. The irresistible implication at present is that the Church appointed a committee to discover the truth, discovered it, didn't like it, and is now trying to cover it up again.

It is not my wish or purpose to attack the Church of England, the letters C. of E. are stamped upon my identity disc, and the atmosphere of my own parish church is more congenial to me than that of other denominations'. My main wish is to explain why so many men of honest intellect have become estranged from the Church, particularly in connection with this question of personal survival.

A good deal of unhappiness is caused to believers in the literal truth of the Creeds by the thought that their dear ones may be lying in an indefinite coma little different from death itself so far as existing conditions are concerned: and, as I shall try to show later, there is evidence of widespread grief and despondency among spirits recently departed from this life, because, although they can see and mingle with those left behind, they cannot communicate to them that all is well, nor assuage their grief.

If it were to become a matter of common acceptation that the existence of the spirit is substantially uninterrupted by death, and that existence and consciousness are in fact continuous, much unhappiness would be avoided by the living and the dead.

Of course this fact has no direct connection with the Church, Christianity or any other religion; but the present attitude of the Church is an important hindrance to an unbiased examination of the evidence, and to an acceptation of the facts if such examination makes it appear reasonable to suppose that they are as stated above.

Naturally the doctrine of the Resurrection of the Body is not the only thing which estranges modern intellectual men from the Church. A very important factor is the exclusiveness of the Churches, which is epitomised in the story of the old Scotswoman: "Why, Mrs. Fraser, I believe you think that nobody will be saved except you and your Minister."

"Aye, but whiles I hae ma doots aboot the Meenister." Gibbon tells us that, before the Nicene Council, no creed had been drawn up as a test of orthodoxy, although there were various formulae of Christian belief in various places for the use of candidates for admission to the Christian community.

The introduction of a creed, so far from allaying misunderstanding and enmity, led to a period of savage recrimination between the Christian sects, and they assailed one another with an intensity and malevolence which had never been displayed by the tolerant and rather contemptuous Romans in their persecutions of a wayward sect. Ammianus wrote that the enmity of Christians towards each other surpassed the fury of savage beasts against man.

This ferocious interpretation of the religion of Love persisted until comparatively recent times, and although we no longer apply the axe and the thumbscrew as the weapons of Evangelism, a legacy of suspicion and bitterness remains which tends towards a continuing estrangement of the Churches and imposes an obstacle against their combination in a common cause.

This exclusiveness is probably a legacy from Judaism and the idea of the Chosen Race, but the idea is repugnant to many intellectual men, who may think that a good Buddhist is nearer to the Kingdom of Heaven than a bad Christian.

Then again, the evidence for the detailed accuracy of the Gospel stories is very slender, and it is possible for an extremist to maintain that the evidence even of Christ's existence upon earth would be unsatisfactory to a conscientious historian engaged in secular research, though there are not many who would follow him to that length. The doctrine of the Trinity came from India and Egypt and was expounded by Plato more than three hundred years before the birth of Christ, His place being taken by the "Logos." A "poetical fixation of these abstractions" sometimes regarded the Logos as the Son of an Eternal Father, and Creator and Governor of the world.

For Heaven's sake don't get the idea that I have any doubt about Christ's existence on earth or about the general truth of the Gospels and of His teaching as set forth therein. I only regard it as a mathematical certainty that, under the conditions in which the Gospels were produced and standardised, some errors at least should have been perpetuated.

The only theory which would entitle us to reject such a conclusion would be that the literal accuracy of the Gospels was ensured by the Divine inspiration of the authors. This theory cannot be maintained in face of the manifold contradictions and differences between the Gospels. Luke, for instance, gives 42 generations between David and Joseph, while Matthew gives 26. And why labour the pedigree of Joseph at all if it is maintained that he was not the father of Jesus? Also it seems to me in the highest degree presumptuous for mortal man to attempt to set forth in black and white the mysteries of Divine attributes, which could not be comprehended by our three-dimensional minds even if they were accurately known.

Again, the only theory which would justify the meticulous definitions of (for instance) the Athanasian Creed would be the intervention of Divine inspiration. This explanation will not readily satisfy anyone who reads the accounts of the tumultuous assemblies organised by the bemused ecclesiastics of the fourth century.

A slavish belief in the literal truth of the Gospels and the Creeds is not Faith, it is Superstition.

I should define Christian faith under two headings. First, a positive one, an absolute belief in the infinite goodness and wisdom of God, in spite of any evidences of pain, sorrow, evil or apparent mismanagement. Second, a negative one, a refusal to disbelieve in any phenomenon, past, present or future, purely on the grounds that it is impossible. This is a very different thing from compulsion to believe in the truth of remote phenomena in the teeth of evidence indicating the strong probability of their falsity. Rational men are entitled to retain an open mind until they have more knowledge. I here quote an extract from a series of spirit messages with which I shall deal later. At this stage I do not discuss its validity nor the circumstances of its reception; that will come later.

"Whenever men asked what they should do in this case or in that, in order that they should not fail to coordinate their own acts with His will, the answer was "Look backward to Him, and learn of Him." And if any man inquired further where he would be able to find the will of Christ expressed, the answer was that such expression would be found in a book, the book of the records of His acts and words. Naught but what was found therein was to be believed as His will, and on His will as therein expressed the doings of Christendom were shaped.

"And so it came to pass that Christendom became tied with a tether to a book. The Church truly was alive with the life of Him; His Spirit filled it up like the living coursing blood in a human body. But that life was being strangled and the body began to halt, and at last to go round more slowly in that circumscribed orbit.

"Truly His acts and words recorded were a most precious heritage. They were meant to be a Shekinah to guide the Church through the wilderness of the ages. But, note you well, the Shekinah went before the Children of Jacob and led them. The book of the New Covenant did not go before, but was enthroned behind. The light cast was true light, as from a beacon atop of a hill. But it lighted men from behind and threw their shadows before them. If they would look to the light they must turn their glance over their shoulders backwards. Then they stumbled. It is not of orderly advance to be turning backward in order to see how to go forward.

"That was the error men made. 'He is our Captain,' said they, 'and He goes before us and we follow Him through death and resurrection into His Heaven beyond.' But for a sight of this Captain going before them they turned round and looked to their rear, which is not, I say, conducive to orderly advance, nor agreeable with reason." My last point is that certain clerics, confronted with the agonising difficulty of reconciling Christ's teaching with the problems of modern competitive life, have effected the reconciliation by disowning His message. A Dean of the Church of England wrote words to this effect in the *Strand* Magazine of September 1942.

"The Sermon on the Mount is a series of violent paradoxes which are intended to be interpreted in the light of the rest of the teaching and acts of Jesus." It may be said that destructive criticism is cheap; but on the other hand an irresponsible layman may be accused of presumption if he offers unsolicited advice. Still, having said so much, I will set forth my ideas in the hope that they may be of some value, if only as a basis for constructive discussion.

In the first place, I think that the aforementioned report on Survival, and Communication with the dead, should be published; and that a standing committee should be formed to examine and report on fresh evidence as it becomes available, and generally to keep Church opinion informed and up to date.

Next, on the assumption that the findings of the report are positive, prayers for the dead should be introduced as a regular feature of Church of England services. We can both help the dead and be helped by them.

Thirdly, the Church should make an open disavowal of that terrible exclusiveness which is epitomized at the end of the Athanasian Creed: "This is the Catholic Faith: which except a man believe faithfully, he cannot be saved." Lastly I suggest that the Church should announce and teach that an acceptance of the literal verbal accuracy of the Scriptures and Creeds is not essential for membership of the Christian brotherhood, still less for ultimate salvation. Young people think for themselves a good deal nowadays, hence the reluctance of many boys to present themselves for Confirmation. I am sure, too, that many a thoughtful man is deterred from entering the Priesthood by the rigid opinions to which he is compelled to subscribe.

It seems to me that the open mindedness of which such a policy would be an outward and visible sign might be a first step towards a mutual understanding between the Churches, the acceptability of their teachings to intelligent men, and an improvement in the harmony and efficiency of their efforts in the missionary field.

CHAPTER 3

SPIRITUALISM

I ought to begin this chapter by analysing the phenomena of Spiritualism into components which can be conveniently dealt with; but first I must say that with every line I write I feel a sense of my limitations, due to lack of study and personal experience, in tackling such a vital subject. I feel that the implied criticism was a just one when I told a friend that I was starting on this book, and he said good-humouredly, "Where angels fear to tread; eh?" That friend is experienced and is himself a medium, he has already helped me with my work and will help me more, and I nearly took his semi-quotation as the title for this book. But then I thought, "No. There is nothing to be ashamed of. If this book is to serve its main purpose, it must come out soon, while all these lads are having their souls violently torn from their bodies, and leaving inconsolable dear ones behind. There is no time for deep and prolonged study. And another thing— I want to present to my readers my first sharp clear cut impressions before they have been dulled by much chewing of the cud. This is not a learned treatise on Spiritualism; it is an amateur attempt to interest such men as are materialists only because they have never had the opportunity of being anything else. Neither salvation nor knowledge comes by cataclysm; if this book interests them they should pursue the subject by thought, study and discussion on their own account, and then follow the light which they find. So I will go ahead, and the only thing which I will promise to my readers is that I will be intellectually honest with them and with myself." And if my reading is incomplete—if my list of phenomena is not comprehensive, or if my interpretations are unorthodox—let the pundits be patient with me; the outer world knows little of psychic phenomena and usually misinterprets what it does know. Be the reason what it may, the word Spiritualism brings to the mind of the average man a picture of triviality, deceit and intellectual childishness. Let me do what I can to help Spiritualism to get a square deal.

In the book *Spirit Teachings*, to which I shall extensively refer at a later stage, will be found a description of the types of manifestation commonly produced at séances attended by the author of the book and his biographer. Greatly condensed these are:

1. Raps of great variety, and footsteps shaking the room. Raps were distinctive of different spirits and frequently occurred at a distance from the table.

2. Raps which answered questions and spelt out messages by means of the alphabet.

3. Lights, described as objective and subjective. Objective lights could be seen by all present while the subjective lights could be seen only by those of mediumistic temperament.

4. Scents of different descriptions, sometimes poured on to the hands and handkerchiefs of the sitters. "Nearly always found to be oozing out of the medium's head."

5. Musical sounds in great variety. Sounds similar to those produced by musical glasses, a violincello, a hand bell, or a wind instrument between a clarinet and a trumpet. Mostly single notes: no tunes. The explanation given was that the medium was peculiarly unmusical.

6. Writing produced direct by spirit agency and not through the hand of a medium. Chiefly short messages, answers to questions, or greetings.

7. Movements, often irresistible, of heavy bodies such as tables and chairs.

8. The bringing of various objects from other rooms through closed doors.

9. The direct spirit voice (as opposed to the spirit voice speaking through the medium in trance). Never heard clearly or distinctly by this circle, and seldom attempted.

10. The spirit voice speaking through the medium in trance.

Always different in accordance with the identity of the spirit communicating.

It will be noticed that in this list is not included the phenomenon of automatic writing, presumably because this does not require a circle of séance but may be operated in solitude by the medium. Automatic writing is by far the most prolific method of obtaining long and cohesive messages, and most of the communications discussed in this book were obtained by this method.

There is also no mention of the violent phenomena attributed to low grade spirits called poltergeists. These may occur otherwise than at séances, and may be of a dangerous or destructive type. It is stated, for instance, that heavy objects may be hurled through the air to a considerable distance.

There is also the extremely mysterious but apparently well authenticated phenomenon of the production of Ectoplasm—a quasi-material substance which issues from the body of the medium and may be used in the materialisation of spirit forms and in the construction of apparatus for the application of spirit motive-power.

Now I will say straight away that I propose to treat these physical phenomena very summarily—all these lights and sounds and smells and bumps and raps and things that go bump in the night generally. For one thing one must have had personal experience to write about them intelligently; and, for another, this book will be quite long enough if I confine myself to the discussion of intelligible messages and their impact on a rational intelligence.

You are, however, entitled to ask two questions: "Do they, in fact, happen? And if so why should serious and respectable spirits expend their power and energy in producing such apparently childish conjuring-tricks?" In answer to the first question, I should say that the evidence that some such things happen is quite overwhelming. Many scientific investigators have been convinced, and even inexperienced experimenters can often produce results which astonish them (though stern warnings are given against unguided experiments undertaken in a spirit of mere curiosity). I shall not labour this point because the whole gamut of physical phenomena might be proved to be fraudulent or hallucinatory without affecting the purpose of this book.

The second question, however, deserves a more serious consideration. If we eliminate the violence and buffoonery of effects attributed to malicious or undeveloped spirits, we are left with a residue of impressions on four of the five senses, caused by allegedly estimable spirits engaged in the task of conveying important truths to mankind across the gulf which is fixed between the quick and the dead. As I understand it, the explanation given is that this world is now sunk in a slough of materialism, and that the apparently miraculous stimulation of any of our senses is of value in impressing on mankind the existence of spirits and their power of communicating with us; and that this will tend to reduce scepticism concerning the spiritual origin of messages which might otherwise be attributed to fraud or self-deception on the part of the medium.

Well, there you are! Perhaps I am not a good, counsel for the defence, but it is the best explanation I have seen so far, and it is apparently corroborated by the willingness of the transmitters of serious and important messages to work small miracles in order to convince a doubting medium of their authority and power. (I shall quote one such specific incident in my final chapter.) If I say that I propose to ignore physical phenomena, however, I don't infer that they are unworthy of attention. The pursuit of knowledge for its own sake is a worthy aim, and often results in unexpected practical benefits.

It is true that Science is handicapped in its investigation of psychic phenomena by the restricted conditions in which they are normally manifested. For instance, darkness is often claimed to be an essential requirement, and undue interference by investigators may cause serious harm to the medium.

Still, there is plenty left to work on. If a table can be lifted by power flowing from hands which are in a position to exert only downward pressure, there is something for Science to investigate and explain. Visible lights can presumably be analysed by the spectroscope, and perfumes can be chemically examined at leisure.

The wave-lengths of known etheric vibrations vary between a tiny fraction of a millimetre and a distance of over a mile: we have instruments capable of detecting vibrations at various stages between these limits: does the psychic "power" give readings on any of these instruments? If not, can instruments be devised to measure the intensity and wave length of the vibrations? I am not here suggesting that spirit power can be harnessed for the operations of daily life, though perhaps stranger things have happened even than this. A more practical speculation would perhaps be that an increased knowledge of psychic mechanics might result in an improvement in the means of communication between the two worlds. Mediumistic qualities are comparatively rare in mankind, and are not necessarily associated with high mental development. Furthermore it is reasonable to suppose that spirits may not reach a state of profound knowledge until they have left the earth for so long that they have become out of touch with it and consequently have great difficulties to overcome in establishing communication.

You know that, at the moment when you read these lines, the space around you is filled with vibrations which make absolutely no impression on any of your senses; yet, if you have a radio set, you can pick out of the ether anyone of hundreds of messages which are being simultaneously transmitted. It does not do violence to our reason, therefore, to suppose that out of scientific study might emerge a form of psychic radio which would increase our powers of contact with the spirit world and clarify our communications.

I have no more to say now on this subject. It does not affect my main purpose, which is to discuss the validity and value of the messages allegedly received from spirits. I have dealt with it at this length because the apparent triviality of psychic phenomena deters many people from any contact with spiritualism, and it is only fair to show that apparently puerile manifestations may have a wise and beneficent purpose.

Recently I was rash enough to tell a foolish woman that I was writing a book on spiritualism. She said: "Oh, don't do that, it is so false and wrong" She then went on almost in the same breath to tell me that she lived in a house which had a ghost in every room, and quoted several instances of the intervention of spirits in human affairs. I hope she won't read this, or at any rate that she won't fit the cap on, but if she does she must regard herself as a martyr in the cause of progress, because her attitude epitomises that of a good many people, who firmly believe in the actuality of certain psychic experiences which have occurred to them or to their friends, but yet are prepared to stigmatise as superstitious and dangerous rubbish all accounts of the experiences of others.

If you believe that in one single instance a spirit has survived bodily death and has been able to communicate with the living, if only by means of a rap, you have surrendered your basic position as a sceptic, and you ought to be interested in following an inquiry into the evidence regarding the future experiences of your own soul.

And so I put you aside for the moment while I talk to those others who maintain that no such instance has occurred ever, or at any rate since the end of that nebulous era entitled the "Age of Miracles." Now, as I have already said, personal experience is the only evidence which will bring conviction to the determined sceptic; but I am not exaggerating when I say that there are hundreds of instances where the evidence of survival and communication is easier to accept than the alternative theories of fraud, self deception, or the workings of that mysterious agency, the subconscious mind.

It is the passionate desire to give absolute evidence of authenticity which lends an air of triviality or even of flippancy to so many messages. "Do you remember the time when we found Uncle Fred's whisky bottle in the linen cupboard?" is the type of message which will carry to the recipient complete conviction of the identity of the transmitting personality, but nobody would call it elevating or instructive.

It is also reasonable to suppose (and the point is of great importance) that the spirits of those who have recently left this life are in no position to reveal profound truths, because they know little more than they did when they were on earth. They know only that they continue to exist, and, vaguely, that all is well with them, and this is the message which they want to get across to their loved ones left behind. So I shall not occupy any great part of this book in multiplying instances which go to prove nothing but the fact of survival and the possibility of communication. If conviction on these points does not come to you automatically as you read this book I shall be very much surprised; but the important and interesting study is that of the contents of the messages themselves.

Not every spirit message is true—far from it. Errors may arise from ignorance, presumption, malice or irresponsible mischievousness on the part of the communicating spirits, from the fraudulence of mediums (much rarer than is generally supposed), or from defects in the very elaborate mechanism of communication which sometimes seems to be employed.

Before I finish this chapter, I ought to say a word about spiritual healing. I don't mean the faith healing which occurs when a neurotic person, whose illness is largely due to his state of mind, is cured by an alteration of his mental state brought about by the magnetic or forceful personality of the individual who treats his case. I mean sheer latter-day miracles. The rapid recovery of persons suffering from incurable maladies, or of those whose lives doctors have given up for lost. It is true that these cures normally have nothing to do with spirit messages, except in so far as the healer may be directed to the patient, or vice versa, by supernormal methods. Their relevance is more on a par with that of the physical manifestations of spiritualism, and their object may be conjectured to be a reinforcement of other phenomena tending to break through the hard-shelled materialism of the Western world and to open men's eyes to possibilities which they have hitherto ignored.

Be that as it may, the evidence for these miracles is quite conclusive unless we assume a widespread conspiracy among responsible medical men and scientists.

The evidence for the "Miracles of Lourdes" is well documented, and there are at the present moment faith healers, operating in this country, whose cures can only be described as miraculous. One of them is a dear friend of my own and I should like to give some account of his work. I have been asked, however, to hold my hand for the time being, although I hope at a later date to be privileged to describe some of his methods and results.

CHAPTER 4

BIBLIOGRAPHY

Now I want to devote a short chapter to outlining my proposals for the structure of the rest of this book and telling you about my sources of information. (Incidentally I am afraid that I must expose how small a fraction I have assimilated of the available literature on the subject into which I have so boldly plunged; but I have already apologised for my temerity.) My first task must be to try to convince you of the fact of survival, the possibility of communication and the fact that it actually occurs. As I have said, I shall not occupy very much space with this, because it is only necessary to prove a single case to prove the whole so far as survival and the possibility of communication are concerned. The book which I shall choose for the purpose is *Raymond*, by Sir Oliver Lodge (Methuen, 1916). I choose it because it is widely known and because of the eminence of its author in the scientific world.

Then there are a number of books which purport to contain messages from spirits who have left this earth a comparatively short time before the dates of their communications. While, therefore, the authors of the messages cannot be expected to have attained such knowledge and experience as would qualify them to instruct us in the deeper mysteries of the future life, they can supply a mass of information from which we may extract a reasonably good idea of what is likely to happen to us, and people like us, when we come to die. I say "people like us" because the evidence seems to show that people of one language or habit of thought naturally gravitate into one another's company, and furthermore that their thought and will-processes have a good deal to do with their surroundings, in fact to some extent they create their own environment. Congo negroes, or Eskimos, would gravitate together in entirely different surroundings; and there is nothing to repel the intellect in the idea that, after various periods of development, all tributary streams of progress may unite in a single river.

These comparatively elementary books are: *The Eternal Question*, by Allen Clarke. (Dent, 1919.) Mainly useful as a reinforcement to Raymond in carrying conviction concerning survival and communication.

Private Dowding with notes by W. T. P. (J. M. Watkins.) Messages from a private killed in the last war. The fact that his name is the same as my own is a pure coincidence; I had no knowledge of his existence a month ago. The book is valuable not only as giving the experiences of a soldier killed in action, but because it gives an interesting account of the progress and development of a spirit in the early stages of its discarnate career.

The Triumph of Life Eternal. (J. Dinsdale, 47, Westfield Road, Leeds 4.) A series of messages received by Mrs. Gascoigne, C.B.E., and her daughter through her late husband, Colonel Gascoigne, whose present work consists mainly in organising the system by which the spirits of men killed in this war are met and guided.

It is of absorbing interest and poignancy and I shall later quote from it extensively.

The Scripts of Cleophas, by Geraldine Cummins. (Rider.) A detailed history of the early Church written under automatic control by a lady whose education and interests lay in quite other directions. This book is chiefly useful as evidence of the authenticity of communication, though it is very interesting.

Do the Dead Live? by Paul Heuze (Murray) is a translation from the French of an account by a journalist of his experiences while executing a commission to elicit the views of those best qualified to speak on "Spiritualism" in prance. He was on the staff of L'Opinion, which gave him his commission. His conclusions may be described as indefinitely negative, but he issues sensible warnings against the dangers of amateur "spirit-hunting" and pokes some slashing fun at the result of the sport.

(After Death: Letters from Julia), by W. T. Stead. (Stead, Bank Buildings, W.C.2.) These are letters from a comparatively immature spirit ardently pressing those on earth to help in breaking down the barriers which exist between the two worlds. Her later messages are more advanced.

Letters from the Other Side, by Henry Thibault. (Watkins.) A spirit named Philemon replies to a series of questions. He speaks as one having knowledge and authority and the book is a useful cross check on other messages.

Now we come to the most important of my books of reference: *The Life Beyond the Veil*, by the Revd. G. Vale Owen. (Thornton Butterworth.) I say that it is the most important because it purports to give a more or less comprehensive account of a spirit's progress from the time when he leaves his body until he has arrived at a stage of development beyond which conditions are so remote from earth life that they cannot be mirrored in words which would have any meaning to us. Vale Owen's book will supply the framework on which I shall attempt to build a general picture of what a student of these books might expect to find on the other side of death.

Next comes a book called *Letters from a Living Dead Man*, by Elsa Barker. (Rider.) This is a most disturbing book, because, although it gives a graphic picture of life in the regions closest to earth, and one which is not inconsistent with other accounts, it violently contravenes in almost every respect the pictures which we may have formed of later developments. If I hadn't promised to be intellectually honest, I should like to pretend that I hadn't read it, and leave it out of this book, but as matters stand it shall have a section to itself.

Finally there is what I may call the Spiritualists' Bible. *Spirit Teachings*, by W. Stainton Moses. (London Spiritualist Alliance.) It consists of a series of messages from spirits claiming high authority and deep knowledge. These messages purport to correct for us Christians the mistakes in our beliefs and the errors in our Scriptures, and are, therefore, obviously of the greatest importance.

They form however an entirely separate compartment in this book, because my main purpose in writing it is to build a composite picture of the after life as revealed in the books with which I have dealt, in the hope that those who see the picture as one acceptable to the intelligence may lose the fear of death in the anticipation of a rational and happy afterlife, and that the dead may be serene in the knowledge that those left behind realise that all is well with their spirits.

The second stage of my ambition is that I may be privileged to add my mite towards the great work of attacking the entrenched materialism of the age.

For neither of these purposes is it necessary to preach a new religion, still less one which will cut at the roots of some of the beliefs which

Christians hold most dear. However, I am getting ahead of my horses: Stainton Moses and "Imperator" shall have a chapter to themselves at the end of the book.

Other books from which quotations are sparingly made are: *Through the Mists* and *The Life Elysian*, by R. J. Lees, and *Letters from Lancelot*, by R. M. T.

CHAPTER 5

PROOF OF SURVIVAL

I think that *Raymond* is a very important book because its main purpose appears to be to convey to the world proof of human survival after death. This proof is conveyed by the publication of a series of messages from Raymond Lodge, the son of Sir Oliver Lodge, the famous scientist and author of the book. Sir Oliver claims to show beyond reasonable doubt that he and his family were in fact in communication with Raymond and no other, because certain items of information were received. This information would be known to Raymond and to certain members of his family, but would be unknown outside the immediate family circle, and certainly unknown to the mediums through whom the majority of the messages were transmitted.

This desire to establish proof of identity runs through the whole series of messages, and Raymond himself eagerly enters into the spirit of the enterprise; so much so that, long after Sir Oliver and the more sceptical members of his family have been completely convinced of the reality of the communications and the identity of Raymond, tests and cross checks continue to be devised.

Raymond was Sir Oliver's youngest surviving son, born in 1889.

At the outbreak of war 1914 he was an electrical and mechanical engineer in his brothers' works, and, although he had no personal or family association with military life or ideas, he volunteered for service in September, 1914, and was gazetted as a 2nd Lieutenant in the South Lancashire Fusiliers. His battalion went to Flanders in March, 1915, and he was killed in action near Ypres in September, 1915, at the age of 26.

The first message which Sir Oliver received in connection with the death of his son was a premonitory one emanating from a distinguished psychic investigator named Myers who had died in Rome when Raymond was about twelve years old. The message was received in America on August 8th, 1915, and intimated that Sir Oliver was about to receive a heavy blow, but that he (Myers) would operate to soften and mitigate its effects. References to Myers and his association with Raymond in the afterlife are frequent throughout the book.

The next piece of evidence adduced by Sir Oliver is that descriptions were received, from two mediums independently, of a group photograph taken in France, in which Raymond appeared.

The photograph was described, in messages purporting to emanate from Raymond, before the negatives reached England where the prints were made.

Later messages describe Raymond's work (helping those killed in action through the first stages of their new consciousness) and tell of his meeting with a sister who had died in extreme infancy, and with a brother who had never drawn the breath of life. These have both reached maturity. He makes little jokes, e.g., "a Roland for your Oliver," meaning that Sir Oliver had recently acquired a son-in-law named Rowland. He gives his own nickname and that of a brother. He gives the names of songs which he used to sing.

At a certain sitting he shows detailed knowledge of what had happened at a previous sitting with a different medium in another place.

He describes a lopsided bathing tent (broken in a gale and mended by the family) at the seaside, and a "sand yacht," running on wheels, which he and his brothers had spent many hours in building. He asks: "Do you remember a bird in the garden?"

"Do you remember Mr. Jackson?"

"Put him on a pedestal." Mr. Jackson was the name of Lady Lodge's peacock which had just died.

He was to be stuffed, and Lady Lodge had shown the taxidermist a wooden pedestal on which the bird was to be mounted.

The messages were mostly received through various mediums, but some came through "table tilting" in the family circle. These last were intimate and almost boisterous affairs as if Raymond were in the room and skylarking with his family (e.g., trying to make the table climb up on to the sofa).

"All very trivial," perhaps you say, "and unworthy of the attention of students of a serious subject." Yet I don't know that I should quite agree with you. If the intention of the messages was to carry conviction of survival and identity, it would be just these little family jokes and memories which would be emphasised.

The messages were by no means all of this nature. Some of them gave details of Raymond's life and surroundings, and there was one message, suppressed by Sir Oliver from the highest motives, which indicated that Raymond was privileged to witness one of those Manifestations which, as will be seen later, appear to constitute no uncommon element in the education of the afterlife.

These messages will be more appropriately mentioned as cross references later on when I am trying to build up a composite picture of life after death from the materials at my disposal; but there is one item which must be dealt with at some length here, because it is a ridiculous detail which has wrecked the whole credit of the book with superficial readers, or rather with those who read nothing but prefer to form dogmatic opinions at second hand. I refer to the mention of cigars, and whisky-and-soda in the afterlife.

People say "Raymond" is supposed to drink whisky-and-soda.

There cannot be any whisky-and-soda in the afterlife. Therefore the book must be rubbish, and a distinguished scientist like Sir Oliver Lodge must be suffering from senile decay, or else he would never have allowed it to appear over his name." In the first place, since accuracy has its value even in controversy, it may be just as well to see what was said. This is the passage: "He says he doesn't want to eat now. (He is Raymond; the medium is speaking.) But he sees some who do; he says they have to be given something which has all the appearance of an earth food.

People here try to provide anything that is wanted. A chap came over the other day, he would have a cigar. 'That's finished them,' he thought. He means he thought they would never be able to provide that. But . . . they were able to manufacture what looked like a cigar. He (Raymond) didn't try one himself, because he didn't care to; you know he wouldn't want to. But the other chap jumped at it. But when he began to smoke it he didn't think so much of it; he had four altogether and now he doesn't look at one. They don't seem to get the same satisfaction out of it, so gradually it seems to drop from them. But when they first come they do want things. Some want meat and some strong drink, they call for whisky-sodas. Don't think I'm stretching it, I tell you that they can manufacture even that. But when they have had one or two they don't seem to want it so much—not those who are near here. He has heard of drunkards who want it for months or years over here, but he hasn't seen any. Those I have seen, he says, don't want it anymore." Now all this certainly seems very odd at first sight, but it all hangs together with the idea, which is inherent in all the messages dealing with the subject, that the personality and mentality of spirits when first leaving the human body is quite unchanged, and that they commonly fail for some time even to realise the fact that they are dead. It is no good making up one's own ideas about the next world, and then rejecting evidence simply because it does not it in with those ideas.

The Living Dead Man, for instance, has a most amusing chapter about a woman who still lives in a boarding house, eats three meals a day, and complains of the coffee. And Private Dowding knows a quaint old French editor who has made himself a nice little office, full of typewriters and tape machines, from which he watches with absorbed interest the progress of his beloved paper under the management of his son.

All these puerilities, of course, only attach to those spirits who have no desire to progress beyond their earthly ideas; and I should guess that in most cases the phase is purely temporary.

The Scripts of Cleophas is mentioned here chiefly as evidence of the reality of communication. The messages came to a lady who played hockey for Ireland, whose education was in no sense classical, and whose interests lay in quite other directions.

The book purports to reveal the contents of three early Christian parchments, long since destroyed. It has been submitted to eminent Hebrew scholars who are impressed by the wealth of detailed knowledge disclosed. Quite apart from its evidential value for my purposes, it is of absorbing interest for its own sake. It gives a detailed account of the character of the apostles and their vicissitudes in the early days after the Crucifixion. It, and its companion volumes, *Paul in Athens* and *The Great Days of Ephesus*, show St. Paul in a kindlier light than that shed on him by the "Acts" or by his own Epistles.

The Eternal Question is a book calculated to bring conviction concerning the facts of Survival and Communication, rather because of the homely nature of its contents, than because of any circumstantial revelation of life after death. The author was a journalist and the editor of a small paper in the Northern Midlands. He married and lost his first wife (V-) after only four months of happy married life. He was a free thinker and a strong opponent of Spiritualism, which he frequently denounced in his articles.

His second wife (E-), unknown to either of them, was a strong medium, and after the death of one of their children she fell into a series of trances in which the first wife, V-, appeared with the dead baby. These trances occurred sometimes at inconvenient moments and places, and E-used to fall down unconscious in conditions which were very alarming, although she was never on any occasion injured in the least degree.

The last trance communication from V occurred at the house of some friends when the author wanted to catch the last train home. Consequently V-was somewhat brusquely repelled by a fellow-guest, and she never again came in circumstances where communication could be made.

A spirit-photograph and many other psychic experiences are included, but the main value of the book perhaps lies in the humdrum setting of the events, and it may carry conviction to those who have an ineradicable suspicion of paid mediums.

I might add that, pending the publication of the report referred to in Chapter 2, it is perhaps not unreasonable to adduce as confirmatory evidence of Survival and Communication the action of the Church of England in suppressing the results of its own inquiry into these matters.

This is all that I propose to adduce in the way of direct evidence —not from lack of material but from lack of space. I ought, however, in fairness to the materialist to give an explanation which purports to cover the automatic receipt of messages dealing with subjects unknown to the recipient, or indeed to any person on earth, without admitting the agency of discarnate spirits. If I may take as representative the explanation proffered in the Introduction to the *Gate of Remembrance*, by F. B. Bond (who conducted excavations at Glastonbury Abbey), the theory is as follows: "The embodied consciousness of every individual is but a part, and a fragmentary part, of a transcendent whole, and within the mind of each there is a door through which Reality may enter as an Idea—Idea presupposing a greater, even a cosmic Memory, conscious or unconscious, active or latent, and embracing not only all individual experience and revivifying forgotten pages of life, but also Idea involving yet wider fields, transcending the ordinary limits of time, space and personality." This explanation can be made to cover the case of a charwoman producing a script in Sanskrit; and you must judge for yourself whether its acceptance does not involve a greater strain on the credulity and imagination than the acceptance of the simpler notion that discarnate spirits are sending messages to people on earth.

But, however received, the messages remain on record, whether transmitted by intelligent beings, or extracted by a lucky dip from the Cosmic Vat. It is my task to examine and correlate these messages, and not to enter into endless discussion about their origin.

You may think that the composite picture which they present is altogether false and misleading, you may have your own ideas about the future life, but you cannot be sure that you are right, and if you should find that, after all, the progress of the spirit is more or less on the lines which appear to emerge from these messages, then you will not find yourself in a state of complete lostness and bewilderment, and you will be glad that you have read this book.

CHAPTER 6

DEATH ON THE BATTLEFIELD

A s a contrast to the somewhat sterile attempt to prove the facts of Survival and Communication by argument, I should like you to read the following messages which have all come from men killed in action during the present war. They came to Mrs. Gascoigne and her daughter through the agency of the late Colonel Gascoigne who is organising the first spiritual contacts with those who die in battle. Colonel Gascoigne was with the force attempting to relieve Khartoum when it fell, and he was also associated with Cecil Rhodes in the early days of Rhodesia.

Only two or three of the men had known the Gascoigne's in life, but they were so to speak "introduced" by the Colonel. Most of the messages are contained in the last chapter of *The Triumph of Life Eternal*, but a few are now published for the first time.

From a sailor, the son of an old friend.
I was in an oil tanker and we were all drowned when she was hit, it was very quick and I did not suffer any pain but tremendous surprise at finding myself possessed of the most wonderful strength and able to heave away all kinds of wreckage; I was making my way through the debris when I realised that we were moving through deep water. It was so still that it was just like a dream. I remember feeling it was quite easy to move and there was no difficulty in breathing (if we

were breathing), but now I come to think of it, it was a different sort of breath. Anyhow I got free and so did some of my friends and we moved away without quite knowing what we were doing. We found a stranger had joined us, his clothes were quite dry and he walked through the water without it seeming to touch him. I noticed this and after a time I said something to him about it.

It all seemed so queer, and as we walked and walked I saw that we were going towards what looked like a sunrise, the best I've ever seen, and I turned to look back over the way we had come, and the stranger put his hand on my shoulder and said: "Not yet, you must go on out of the Valley of the Shadow of Death and then you can return if you want to." I said, "Oh, I don't care," and I went on in a dazed sort of way until we came to a kind of garden, but it wasn't enclosed, it was on the hillside with lots and lots of flowers; oh, they were lovely. By this time I had realised that we were not walking in the water any more and I felt so tired and sleepy, and my feet refused to go any further, and the stranger suggested that we should rest. I sat down on the grass and was soon asleep.

You cannot imagine my astonishment on waking to find myself in a strange place, and I couldn't at first remember how I got there; but it came back after a time, and I found some of the others, and they let me piece it together with their help. But all the time the stranger stayed with us, and he listened but said nothing, so at last I asked him where he came from, and why he'd brought us here, and he said: "Oh, I'm just a seaman like you, but I've been ashore for some time now, so I thought I might be able to help you." Then, very slowly, we all knew that we were what we used to call "dead," but it was so different that I couldn't believe it.

It's grand, just GRAND. I wish my Mother could know about it.

We are in a far better land than the one we left, and it's all O.K. I'd love her to see it. Dad came to me soon after I realised this and we had a great time together. It seems queer to call him Dad, he's younger than I am now, at least he looks it. We are to have a job together soon, but I am not to be in a hurry.

From a New Zealander.
Can I try? I do not find it difficult, but what is the use of trying? You do not know my people, they are far away and would never understand. I am one of the Colonial troops and my name is Simson.

I came from New Zealand. I guess some of the lads have had their fill of fighting, but that was what we came for, and I am glad I came. I know it wasn't much use in the ordinary way, but we showed our loyalty to Britain, and that's the spirit that will prevail in the end. I was one of the casualties in Greece. I feel I should go home now, but I can't leave my mates. I could go as swiftly as a thought, and return equally quickly, but time doesn't matter now, and if I let go the contact with our lads I may find it difficult to pick it up again. I feel we can do something here now, and if that's so, let's go on doing it.

I am rather vague as to who is "alive" and who is "dead," they all look much alike, but the "dead" are far more active and don't get tired, It seems strange, but I sort of expected this when I came over. I knew I should never go back alive. But my parents would never understand how much more alive I am now, so it's no use my trying to tell them.

I am going straight on with my job, under my own officer, and with many of my pals; we work for the rest, especially when they are asleep, sometimes we raid the enemies "dead" battalion, fighting with our thought weapons! It's a grand game. There are so few things we can't do now. One of the strangest things is that we all feel happy. I wasn't one of the naturally happy ones on Earth. I worried and fidgeted and found time lagged more than most people. But here there is a sort of carefree feeling, and no time to lag, so I can't work up any regret over leaving my body. I stay right here. Our boys are happy, too, all of them, and the others are having such a rough time that it's up to us to stay by them.

Q. Can we help you? Do you need our help? Well, yes, we do. It's ever such a help to do this, it kind of gives me more pep to get into closer touch with my pals. It would be much better if you could have a talk with more of us. You give us confidence.

So often we cannot see the result of our work, but now I can feel and see your reactions, and it makes real work, like I expect it does for you.

Something to show for it. Thank you ever so much. I think that's all for now. Goodnight.

Gunner Simson.

From a Norwegian.
Frankly, I feel rather strange doing this, but it goes quite easily. I I am not English, nor even British, I am a Norwegian. I have lived in

England for many years and I find your language as easy as mine own.

I was shot by the Germans in Trondheim. I was a little shop-keeper; they shoot. I do not love the Germans. I never shall, but I am held up here by my hatred. I find that I cannot throw it off. I still feel so angry for their acts of unprovoked cruelty, and I am consumed with my passionate anger, and cannot get free. I beg of you to help me; your Father he bring me to you to make a closer link with him. He tell me that we must forgive the Nazis, that they do not know what they do, that they are like sleep-walkers, and until I forgive them I cannot get free, to pass from this plane so near the Earth on to other planes.

Here all that happens with you is known and felt in a greater form, and we go on feeling more and more animosity against the German race, and when they join us in the astral body we feel far more antagonism than we felt during our Earth life. It is awful, this anger that we cannot shake it off. Give me serenity and let me sleep. I want to sleep and forget them. I might be fairer in my judgment and come to forgive.

I see why Christ quickly forgave everyone before He left the Earth Body. I see the reason and the need, and with the help of your Father and this contact that you have given me, I shall escape.

J. Ammussen.

A Highlander taken prisoner in Crete.
Yes, I was in Crete. I'm a Highlander. I was in the Marines and I stayed on in Crete among those who couldn't be taken off. It was one of the worst moments when I saw the ships and knew it was hopeless for us to hope for any escape. I got hit in the shoulder, and there was nothing for it but to give in and let them take me prisoner. I was put on to a stretcher and taken to hospital, but they did nothing for me except to give me a bed to lie on, and my wound got septic and very painful. I got delirious I suppose, and they came and questioned me, but I don't think they did anything for me, perhaps they couldn't. I don't know; anyway after ages and ages of suffering I seemed to pass into a timeless sleep, and when I woke up there was no pain, and I was out of doors, so I thought I had escaped and I wandered about glad to be free, but I couldn't make sense of it all. I seemed unable to walk properly, I couldn't keep on the ground, and though I didn't fall it was extremely difficult to move along, and then the whole place would grow misty, I would see places and

people one moment and the next I saw something quite different, I thought I was delirious again. Now I know that I was teeing two planes at once, and I hadn't learnt to manage my spirit body, it all worried me a lot and I got quite hopeless. People would come up to help me, and just as we were beginning to understand each other I Would see the outline of Crete, and be overcome by the desire to hide away from the Germans, it was a sort of torture, and then at last they got through to me and I was able to sleep—the real sleep of death—the putting off of our life and the taking on of another. I don't know much about it, but this life seems so natural that I was anxious to try and write through you so as to test my power on the physical plane before going hack to help those who have suffered like I did. I know we can and I don't want to waste time. It's grand finding that nothing was wasted.

I have all the faculties now that I longed to have on earth. Oh, it's simply grand. Goodnight.

Two letters from a Polish pilot who spent his last leave with us.
Yes, I am shot down and out. I have survived many fights, but not this one. I am wounded, I cannot control the aircraft, it was my leg, you feel the pain, I could not move the controls and I fall, I cannot leave the aircraft, I fall quite consciously. I get up without any pain, I see my observer and gunner, he is hurt too but not so much. The Germans come to find us, they do not see me, I run and hide, but they not look for me, my friend they take away; I wander about, I feel well and cannot think how I came to crash aircraft. My leg is healed. I wander about, I go to the French peasants and ask for help, but they do not see me, and I begin to wonder, I am neither hungry nor thirsty nor particularly tired.

I begin to see things changing, I see first colours everywhere, it is sunset, or sunrise, and it looks as if the colours were reflected in the earth as well as in the sky. I lay and watched the colour take form, it was like a cinema when one picture fades out and another takes its place. I was astounded, I do not know where I am. I ask, I pray, I forget that I have no faith in religion, I pray for help and it comes to me. Someone looking very strange and yet quite like ourselves comes to me, he tells me not to mind the change it is best for all and that I shall be happy in this land.

I am very confused, I think I am taken prisoner, then he explains that there are no prisons or prisoners and I feel free again. He took me away and he told me to sleep, he touched my eyes and I sleep at once. When I wake he is still there and I am on earth again in the occupied territory with Germans all round. I have come back to my body. I find it difficult to leave it.

I see no colours, but my new friend is there too, and he talks to me, but I can't see him well. They are doing something to my body, I am miserable, so my friend tells me to think very hard of some place outside the war, so I think very hard of the last time I see family life with you at H-, I see you all quite easily, and I wake you and you feel me near and you talk to me, I ask you to let me stay and just sit quietly in your house far from the battle until I can go on, and you say "Yes," so I stay, and now I begin to feel sleepy again. I am between the worlds, help me to throw off this one and to go on. I want to go on—I want to go on —I think I can, please help me.

S. Z.

Several days later.
Thank you, yes I am well, I do not yet feel ready to leave your home for very long at a time, but I go for a short time, but it is good to come back to you all. I have strange feelings when you sit in the same chair in which I sit, I am close and yet not close at all.

I am going now sometimes to Poland, but I dare not stay. I have no strength yet to help them, and they need this power so badly; I see my old friends, some dying and some dead, but I can do nothing, I am tired, and feel too ill to reach them. We must help soon, but at present we are too weak.

Your Father, or someone like, he comes with me and we try to help but I am nearly useless, I want to help but I am like a child, I cannot.

Also I never had any faith, nothing to expect on dying, and I am lost, I know nothing. All the things I made fun of come back to me. I was a bad man, I neglected many things, my prayers and my church, but I do not know if that mattered. I had no creed, and now I find that extinction being impossible I have to suffer a sort of conscious extinction, knowing and feeling, and yet being empty of strength.

What you expect here, that you find, you build your awakening, it is just as you imagined, at least that is what they told me. I expected nothing, so nothing came. But now I am pulling out of the difficult doldrums, and am beginning to feel my strength. Thank you for helping.

S. Z.

A letter from a Tank Officer.

Thank you, I am alive after all, I thought extinction was the only thing that could follow such an inferno. We seemed to go down on all sides British and German alike, tanks and guns and planes, I had the feeling that we were being exterminated by the machines of our own creation, they seemed so much stronger and more vindictive than the humans inside them. I believe it's the battle of the machines, they are in charge and we are the slaves of some evil genius through whom they have been created. I feel the influence of evil so strongly, I longed to get away and lie in the clean sand and forget the horrors of man's inferno of which we did not seem to be in charge.

I prayed for help when we stuck in the sand and fire broke out, and prayed with all my soul and I knew we couldn't escape, but prayer seemed to strengthen me and I felt that nothing really mattered so desperately, excepting the feeling of evil, and that had receded, I could not name it or explain it in words. It seemed to meet us from the sand and hang all around the tank battle. I felt sick and miserable, and then it passed off and I found myself standing outside the tank talking to my Colonel. He seemed unconscious of the bullets that were raining down upon us, I ran for shelter, but he called me and told me not to bother. He was looking as young as a subaltern and as though he was enjoying the battle.

He took me by the shoulder and said: "Don't you see, Kit, we are dead, and yet far more alive than they are, and we can go on fighting, hampering the enemy, throwing dust in his eyes, putting ideas into our leaders and playing an invisible hand." I saw that he was serious but I thought he was mad, I said: "Yes, Sir, but I'm so tired I don't think I can move any further." He left me and I don't know what happened, but I woke up here with only one idea —to go back to the battle and find him—he wasn't mad, but I was stupid.

Your Father has let me write through you so as to give me the strength from the physical plane to grapple with the unseen world. I'm off now, thanks a lot—
February 4th, 1942.

Here are two people who would like to write:
Yes, I am very glad to have this chance. I always thought it might be so, but until I was picked off by a Jap sniper, I was never certain.

I fell face downwards in the swampy mud of the jungle, and lay unconscious for a time in a sort of nightmare, my body was trying to reassert itself, and my spirit to get free. Never think that when people are unconscious that they are really so, at least I wasn't. It was a time of conscious paralysis, I hated it, and when something snapped and I was free I was awfully relieved.

I got back to our fellows and I soon realised what had happened when they didn't see me; but I was so interested in finding myself unchanged that I hadn't time to think of anything else. I wanted to tell them not to fear death and all that, but I couldn't. After a time I began to see the Jap dead, they were helping their own fellows, and the living Japs could sometimes see and hear them, and they used all the information given, and this made feel that we should be able to do the same. I tried awfully hard, but I couldn't warn or suggest anything which could be accepted by the brains of our fellows, so I wandered off wondering what to do next.

I didn't exactly want to leave them to it, but there didn't seem to be any alternative, so I did. I wandered off into the forest, and for a time forgot all about the war, and all that my friends were going through because I became so fascinated by the life that I saw all around me. I know the jungle well, I have lived in it alone for months on end, and I came back to it seeking rest and peace after the turmoil of war, and I found all I sought and more—much more. I suddenly found that I was seeing things that had been hidden from me during the whole of my physical life. I cannot describe the beauty of the life around me. The jungle is always rich in colour, sound and beauty of trees and flowers but now behind each thing that I knew so well lurked a hidden meaning, and some beautiful ray or sound seemed to permeate the very texture of the jungle life....

I can't explain. I was superbly happy and entirely myself, but that self had grown in comprehension, and in power to experience contentment and bliss.

Then a voice came to my ears, and gradually I sensed a beautiful shining figure that said to me: "Here you see the land of pure content, but you have left behind a land of passionate unrest. Do you not wish to help others to find the key to this place of joy?" I was so overcome at never having thought of anyone else for ages, that I must have blushed like a schoolboy, but the Shining One didn't seem to notice. So I stammered that I hadn't really grasped my whereabouts yet, and could He help me? He said: "No, you found the way, and the rest you must discover for yourself, but others may not be so fortunate and need helping." I didn't want to turn my back on this glorious place, but the Shining One promised to come with me and not leave me. He explained that I could always return just by recalling this place vividly and wishing myself here, and now equally you and I must see ourselves in the battle zone.

I did most regretfully, and away we seemed to pass, or rather there was no passing, one surrounding faded out and another took shape. The jungle moved or dissolved and its place was taken by another sort of jungle full of men shouting orders and screaming in pain. I felt unable to bear it at first, but the Shining One said: "Come and stand by this man, he is about to pass over to us." A second later and a bullet had ripped through his stomach and he lay groaning at our feet. The Shining One bent down, and touched his head and eyes, and instantly the groaning ceased, and I saw his spirit leave his tortured body, and looking dazed and pale joined us both in the deep foliage of the jungle. Before I knew what had happened we were back in the wonderful jungle; it was a delicious experience. The man who had joined us was one of our own men. A dull, quiet looking fellow. I hardly knew him, he took no interest in games and was always reading. Now he brightened up suddenly upon catching sight of me, and said: "Hello, Sir, I didn't think you'd be here, I thought I'd seen you killed some days ago." I said: "Yes, and I saw you killed some minutes ago." The Shining One looked at me and I knew I shouldn't have broken the news so swiftly. But Burrows didn't seem to mind, "Oh, well, I've copped it have I? Well, I don't care, it's awful fighting here and not much chance of getting out," was all he said. But "What's it like here?" he continued.

I told him it was splendid, and that he had nothing to fear, and we walked about through the jungle clearing while the Shining One explained things to us. Soon we had both recovered from the shock and he took us back to the firing line to fetch more of our people and introduce them to this life. That is where we are now, and I wanted to get further and learn how to impress my thoughts upon the men in charge.

I'm grateful to you for my first lesson; it doesn't seem to have gone too badly, but I'm tired now and I'll wish myself back in my jungle home of refreshment. I see there are no separate places, all are moods within ourselves, just like what we were taught as children. "The Kingdom of God is within you." Goodnight.

February 4th, 1942.

A message came through on January 29th, 1943, from a soldier who was killed in Libya in a skirmish. None of his friends were killed at the same time and he wandered about in a state of great loneliness. The message is less interesting than some of the others, but it contains a very remarkable passage, if you remember our discussion about the Raymond book. There is the quotation: "HOW I longed for a drink I But somehow I couldn't bring myself to do it. But my longing was so strong that I was able to draw the drink I needed. You'll laugh. But I wanted a whisky-and-soda more than anything I've ever wanted in my life, and there it appeared, just like magic, with soda sparkling and clear I poured it out and drank and drank! At first the whisky tasted good, but after a few minutes it was the soda that I wanted clear and clean, and as I wanted it so it changed and became the thing I longed for. But I did not realise that my desire was the factory from which it was being produced." This is a queer coincidence, because I wrote the passage about Raymond's whisky-and-soda two months before I saw this message, which, in fact, has only just arrived in time for insertion during my final revision of the draft of this book.

Another message from Libya:

O. K. I am glad, I've wanted to thank you for some time but I couldn't make you hear.

We came abroad in the Spring. I was one of the Snodsbury lot. I'll give you my name soon but you likely don't remember me. We was all split up and I got sent to Egypt. It was a show, I never thought as how I could have lived through it. You know what I mean. I didn't know that dying was like this. I thought it was all over and finished and sometimes we seemed to go through such a gruelling I didn't see as how we could stand any more, and then all of a sudden it ceased—and I was feeling as upright as a trivet. A moment before I'd been dead beat and hot; oh, hot and thirsty with the most awful headache. The noise of battle fairly shattered me to bits, but then all of a sudden I was cool and fit and fresh as a daisy, and perky as could be, just looking on and hearing the noise, but not feeling shattered by it. I couldn't believe I was a "gonner." I saw my body just holed all over, and yet I couldn't believe it. I think I tried to pull it away from the gun, but there were others on top and beside me all in a heap. We'd got a direct hit all right.

The rest weren't there, that seemed queer to me, none of them, until I saw the officer. He came up to me, I pointed to where his body lay, and he gave a kind of gasp and said: "Oh, well, I suppose that's

that, it's a queer world, Johnson, and I suppose we'd best carry on."
I says: "Yes, Sir, but wot does we do now?"

"Load the gun of course, you blighter," ses he, just as he used to.
I went to obey, but strong as I felt I could not move the shells. They
weren't so heavy as all that, but I could not get a hold of them, they was
slippery, it seemed as though there was a sort of fish scale between my
fingers and the shells. I couldn't hold it. I tell the officer and he comes
to help, cursing proper he was by this time, and the two of us had a
go, but would she budge? Not an inch, it seemed silly like, there was
us two great hefty fellows trying all we knew to lift one small ack-ack
shell and we just couldn't do it. At last I sat down and laughed. "Well,"
I ses, "did you ever hear of two dead blokes firing a gun?"

"Yes, I did," ses he, all angry now and red in the face, "and, wot's
more, we are going to do it. We are fit enough, aren't we? Come on."
So I heaved to again, thinking he'd gone crazy but that it was better
to humour him. So we tried again, and now I begun to see things—
not the efforts we was making with our hands, if you follow me, but
the Captain, he seemed to be sending out power some way, he was
that determined, and I saw him as you might imagine a Call Up station on the wireless (if you could see one) and the answer came not
through his fingers but through himself.

Lots of shadowy people came round us and worked with us, and
the gun wasn't exactly in action, but something was being fired
from her.

Plane after plane came over, and suddenly lost speed, turned for
home or crashed. I was mystified, I couldn't recollect anything like
this, there seemed to be no noise, the discharge was silent, but the
repercussion was distinctly felt by us all, and that seemed to give
us fresh impetus for the next. It was the queerest experience. Just
then I saw Jock coming towards us, he'd stopped a packet too, but
he hadn't been with us before.

He recognized me and the Captain, and saluted and stood ready
for duty; the Captain was too busy to notice him and Jock was always
one for arguing, so I shut him up with "Just you wait and see, Son,
we're learning new operational tactics, us three gonners from the
old batch, so come along and learn and don't interrupt whatever you
do." So I stayed close to Jock and made him watch the Captain.

The Captain was a grand fellow, not a doubt. He seemed to drive
his way through with all his determination against it all, and when I
made to move, he looked up that sharp, and said: "You sit quiet and

think—for God's sake think with all the guts you've got in you, that's wot you must do now. We've got our brains and our determination and if we three hold together we'll pull it off and keep the air protection for our chaps. Don't you see the men who are helping us?" and then I looked and there was Sandy, who got sniped on Thursday, standing waist high in water, making strange movements with his arms. I looked at his eyes, and they were Sandy's, but different, so clear like stars, he seemed inspired, if one could say so I don't think I can finish the story today. May I stop now, and come again? I've loved telling it to you. You see it's my first real adventure. Thank you.

Johnson.

Continuation from O. K.

O. K. I'm all right. I'd like ever so much to finish what I was saying.

Well, as I said, Sandy looked inspired, I can't think of another word, and all at once he seemed to be leading us. and not so much the officer who was following his orders most carefully, and as the shadowy people became clearer, I seemed to lose touch with the live people, and the dead ones seemed more real. Then the Jerries attacked and took the gun and we weren't touched; he came through us without seeing or hearing us, though we could see and hear him and feel the perspiry sense of his nearness. I loathed the smell all of a sudden, though it was familiar enough, it almost made me sick, and I saw Sandy and the officer had moved away. So I pulled Jock up and said: "Don't let's lose sight of those two or we're lost." Jock agreed, but when I got to my feet I found I couldn't stay on the ground; it was most comical and so difficult to move on. I was kind of floating and so was Jock. I said: "Let's hold hands and keep each other down," but instead we seemed to buoy each other up. Oh, we did have a time catching up with Sandy and the Captain, but they didn't notice us, someone else had joined them. He wasn't in uniform and I wondered for a minute how a civilian could have got there; he looked like an Arab, and then when he turned and looked at me, I felt—I felt as though he was re-making me all over again —I knelt down and murmured "Christ" with all the reverence of a child.

"No, not Christ, but a messenger from Him," said the man I was kneeling before, and "He wants you" that was what he said. He wanted me.

"Whatever for?" I gasped out, and I looked up to see where the others were, but I could see nothing but a blinding glorious Light, it seemed to fill my head and burn through something that was keeping me there, and then the voice spoke again, something like this: "By your Sacrifice you have attained to the Crown of Fortitude"— and then I remember no more.

That was the last I saw of Earth. I'd like some of the chaps to know how we pass on—it's a most wonderful thing.

I'm tired now and can't finish. Thank you.

Johnson.

CHAPTER 7

METHODS AND
MESSAGES

N ow I want to say something about the methods of communication by which were received the messages dealt with in this book.

Some of the more intimate "Raymond" messages were received by "table-tilting." The sitters place their hands on a table which moves under power unconsciously emanating from them and controlled by the communicating spirit. Except for arbitrary arrangements, such as one rap for No and three raps for Yes, it is necessary to go through the alphabet for each letter required, the table "recording" its assent when the correct letter is reached. In consequence the method is slow and complicated, and of necessity most of the talking must be done by the sitters. On the other hand, a lower degree of mediumship is demanded by this than by other methods, and Sir Oliver states that a surprising degree of intimacy with the controlling spirit can be attained. (Chapters 10 and 11 and Part 3, Raymond, describe Means of Communication much better and at greater length than I can in this book, and those interested should refer thereto.) Most of the Raymond messages came through professional mediums. The disadvantages of this method are that sittings are generally held in darkness or in a very subdued light, and it is therefore sometimes difficult to get a permanent record of the conversations. A note-taker has to be employed and he sometimes has to work under considerable difficulties.

Another handicap is that the communicating spirit can seldom impress the medium direct.

(Raymond attempted this on one occasion with indifferent success.) The medium in fact has his or her own "Control," or spirit medium on the other side. So we have a threefold transmission: Communicator to Control, Control to Medium, and Medium to Note-taker.

In addition to this, Controls when on earth often belonged to races less materialistic than the Western nations, they may be Asiatics or American Indians whose English is imperfect. The cumulative possibilities of error in the details of messages will therefore be obvious.

Broadly speaking, all the other messages dealt with in this book were received by automatic writing. The sitter takes pencil and paper and tries to empty his mind as completely as possible, when the communicating spirit takes charge and writing begins. The degree of automatism varies considerably. Some sitters are practically unconscious of what they are writing. Others carry on a running conversation with the spirit, sometimes to the annoyance of the latter because the sitter will insist on introducing his own thoughts and objections. Julia was a case in point, she was most severe with poor Mr. Stead, but I shall refer to her messages later.

The "Living Dead Man" brutally controlled his amanuensis at first; so much so that she could scarcely use her hand and arm on the day after a sitting, but later he learned to work through her brain by gentler methods.

Mrs. Gascoigne writes: "The writing is not automatic. We know what we are writing—it is more in my case as if it was being dictated, but I keep my hand entirely off the paper so as to give a free scope. I think you would call it inspirational." Though automatic writing is simpler than transmission through an entranced medium, it is by no means always plain sailing. The number of mediums capable of operating appears to be limited, and it is sometimes necessary to have a transmitting medium on the other side. For instance, when his mother was speaking to the Rev. G. Vale Owen, and later on when three highly developed spirits wished to communicate, they used as a medium a woman who was the guardian of Vale Owen's daughter who had died in infancy.

This is quite understandable as the high spirits in question had long since ceased to talk or think in English, and celestial thought transference had to be converted into English speech.

Another difficulty which pervades the transmission of messages, especially those of the more advanced type, is due to the limitations of our three-dimensional minds, and our restricted ideas of time.

Any conception, for instance, of a system of concentric spheres must be in accordance with our own ideas of Geometry, and consequently liable to error. The imagination, therefore, constantly finds itself in difficulties when attempting to cope with descriptions of the physical geography of the celestial regions.

The Ouija Board or Planchette is a small wooden board, supported on two freely running castors and the point of a pencil. It is operated by power unconsciously emitted from the sitters' hands and controlled by the communicating spirit into written messages.

Its use is scarcely mentioned in the works with which I am dealing.

It was used by Mrs. Vale Owen in an injunction to her husband to submit himself as a channel for spirit communications, but was employed in no other important respect.

There are three more books with which I must deal before I start to build up a composite picture of the future life.

The first of these is *After Death*, more widely known as *Letters from Julia* The messages were received by W. T. Stead, a distinguished literary man at the end of the last century. Among his other activities he was Editor of the *Review of Reviews*. His Preface gives an account of the conditions in which the messages were received, and, if it were possible to carry conviction to sceptics by means of reasoned arguments and detailed instances, this Preface would carry such conviction. It seems, however, that it is not possible to carry conviction by any written statement, since it is always possible to say that the author was dishonest or deluded, and his evidence tainted. In spite of his high reputation, Stead did not escape such calumny. He writes pathetically: "But for this, I should never have persisted in a practice which has brought with it much material loss and no slight discredit. No one who knows anything of the prejudice that exists on the subject will deny that I have no personal interest to serve in taking up the exceedingly unpopular and much-ridiculed position of a believer in the reality of such communications. For years I have laboured under a serious disadvantage on this account in many ways, both private and public. My avowal of my conviction on this matter has been employed in order to discount and discredit everything I have done and said or written. But these disadvantages are as dust in the balance compared with the comfort and consolation I have derived from my communications with those on the other side." Julia Ames died in Boston, U.S.A., in December, 1891. As is not unusual, she had promised a friend, whom she loved as a sister, that she would return after death if possible arid give ocular proof of her continued existence. This she did more than once, making appearances without speech. The friend asked Stead if he thought he could get a message from Julia, and he was immediately successful by means of automatic writing. This led to three series of messages; the first in 1892-3, the second in 1895-7, and the third (unfinished) in 1908.

It is not easy to summarise a whole book in a few words, but this book may be summarised in one—LOVE. There is throughout a passionate insistence on God's Love for all his creatures, and on Julia's conviction that the secret of the Universe is that every creature should bathe in that Love and pass it on to others. That herein lies the remedy, and the only remedy, for all our troubles.

It is true that this book is not so "interesting" as some others in the sense of describing in detail the progress and experiences of the soul and its contacts with others, but it is a paean of praise and glory, and presents an impression of the rapturous happiness of the elect which other more analytical accounts cannot give.

The main preoccupation in the earlier stages of her spirit life is to facilitate communication between the two worlds. She sees the cumulative grief and unhappiness of newly-arrived spirits at being unable to let their loved ones on earth know that all is well in the new life, and she sees the sorrow and despair of those on earth in the absence of any sign from "that bourne from which no traveller returns": and she insistently presses upon Stead the duty of establishing on earth a Bureau by which such communication may be facilitated.

Later on, in 1908, she has modified her opinions to some extent.

She writes: "Although there is the greatest desire to hear from and to communicate with you at first, the desire does not last long under present conditions—Now, after more experience, and with better opportunities for observation, I should say that the number of the "dead" who wish to communicate with the living are comparatively few. . . . Therefore do not think that what I said of the eager, passionate longing of those on this side to communicate with you is true of any but those in the midst of whom I was when I wrote.

But that is no reason why you should not use your best exertions to establish the Bureau—The first importance of the Bureau will be the evidence which it will continually afford of the reality of this world." The Bureau was actually founded and existed for rather more than three years.

In its later stages the book gives some consecutive account of the future state, including some puzzling hints on Reincarnation; but I shall attempt no further summary of its contents, and shall refer to them only as a crosscheck on the general hypothesis which I shall try to present.

The second book which deserves consideration at this stage is *Letters from the Other Side.* As I have stated already, no clue is given as to personalities; the name of the spirit as he was known on earth is withheld at his own request, but, to quote the Preface: "those who knew him on earth as a spiritual guide and friend will recognize him without difficulty." In some ways I think that this is a pity, because the authority of his name as a well-known ecclesiastic would lend weight to his messages, particularly with Churchmen when he criticises the Church—on the assumption, that is, that they were acquainted with the author of the messages and acknowledged their authenticity.

Here is a sample: "I want to say that the Church, our beloved but very faulty, very erring Mother, can only prove and continue to prove a ghastly failure while she retains, unrescinded, the awful doctrine of hopelessness for those who pass on, outside of, or at enmity with, her communion. To the learned we tell the truth.

To the simple, to the little children in the faith, we still deal out the old dogmas, and so drive them to seek refuge, sometimes in very doubtful folds of faith and practice." The feature in which this book differs from most of the others which I have read is that the spirit not only permits, but encourages, the communicator to ask questions, and never tries to evade giving an answer, even to the most difficult.

Other spirits (notably Julia) have their "piece" to speak, and are impatient of interruptions from the scribe, even when the interruption consists of no more than a thought fleeting through the scribe's brain. Philemon (the Celestial name of the author of the Letters) was fortunate in finding a scribe with a mind which appears to have been as nearly inert as is humanly possible. The questioner was not the scribe and so had free play.

Philemon good-humouredly tackles every question flung at him, from the probable duration and outcome of the war (1917) to "Can you learn from Archdeacon Colley how to project writing, and will you do it?" Other questions lead Philemon to discuss books with which we have already dealt. Here is what he says about *Raymond*: — "The impression which I have received about this book is that it is the brave effort of a loving soul recorded by a cautious yet fearless investigator; it resembles the necessary breaking up of the earth, in order, later on, to bring about the beauty and usefulness of smiling cornfields and vineyards. Raymond is an essential step in many persons' advancement at the present stage." To the question "Do you often see Stead?" Philemon replies: "I see Stead seldom. But when we do meet it is a soul feast. He has grown into an awe-inspiring, majestic spirit. He has shed the earthly trammels in a most strange and unusual degree. Stead shed them even on earth, and outlived much that some of us still carry with us through many stages of the new life. I look up to him with reverence, and he loves me and helps me with my work. But he is more universal than I am." It is a fascinating disjointed book; disjointed because of the random way in which the questions are hurled. It rather reminds me of a batsman at the nets, defending his wicket against the assaults of half a dozen different bowlers. I shall say no more about this book except as a crosscheck to the main framework.

The third book, *The Life Beyond the Veil*, forms the backbone of my work. It is the only book I have read which purports to give a consecutive account of the progress of a spirit from the moment of death until the stage is reached where conditions differ so widely from those of this world that they can no longer be described in words which have any meaning to us. This is possible because there are several communicators. The early stages are dealt with by the mother of the scribe (the Revd. George Vale Owen); she died about four years before the messages began. The later stages are described by more highly-developed spirits in accordance with what they state to be a comprehensive plan for the enlightenment of mankind.

G.V.O., as his parishioners affectionately called him, was born in 1869 and educated in Birmingham. He was ordained in 1893 arid was a curate successively in Seaforth and two Liverpool parishes.

In 1900 he was appointed curate-in-charge at Orford, Warrington, where there was then no church. Largely owing to his own exertions a church was built in 1908 and he became the first vicar. He was devoted to, and beloved by, his people, and during the war maintained a regular correspondence with "his lads" who had gone from Orford to serve in the Forces.

This is what he says about the conditions in which the messages came to be written: — "There is an opinion abroad that the clergy are very credulous beings. But our training in the exercise of the critical faculty places us among the most hard-to-convince when any new truth is in question. It took a quarter of a century to convince me—ten years that spirit communication was a fact, and fifteen that the fact was legitimate and good.

"First my wife developed the power of automatic writing.

Then through her I received requests that I would sit quietly, pencil in hand, and take down any thoughts which seemed to come into my mind projected there by some external personality. Reluctance lasted a long time, but at last I felt that friends were at hand who wished very earnestly to speak to me; so, at last, very doubtfully I decided to sit in my cassock in the vestry after Evensong.

"The first four or five messages wandered aimlessly from one subject to another. But gradually the sentences began to take consecutive form, and at last I got some which were understandable.

From that time development kept pace with practice. On two occasions only had I any idea what subject was to be treated. At other times I had fully expected a certain subject to be taken, but on taking up my pencil the stream of thought went off in an altogether different direction." The messages began in the autumn of 1913 and ended in the spring of 1919.

The first volume consists mainly of messages from Vale Owen's mother, and the remaining messages purport to emanate from highly developed spirits (Astriel, Zabdiel and Arnel.) These spirits lived on earth some centuries ago and have long ceased to think in English. It was therefore necessary to employ a transmitting medium on the other side, and for this purpose a woman named Kathleen was chosen. She had been a sempstress in earth life, and was the guardian and guide of Vale Owen's daughter Ruby, who had died in infancy. She became the mouthpiece through which the messages were transmitted.

This is held to account for the archaic English in which the majority of the messages are couched and also for the similarity of the literary style of the different spirits, which is noticeable. On a few occasions Kathleen collects some kindred spirits and writes on her own account. Even so her language remains stilted and pedantic. Vale Owen comments on this, and gets snubbed for his pains.

There are other incongruous points about the messages, and I will try to give you a fair sample later on without suppressing any material objections which an ordinary "sensible" mortal might raise to the credibility of the series.

When the messages were complete, they were published in the Weekly Dispatch between February and December, 1920. Lord Northcliffe wrote a somewhat condescending appreciation, of which the last paragraph is perhaps the most relevant from our point of view. It read "He (Vale Owen) expressed a desire for as little publicity as possible, and declined any of the great emoluments that could easily have come to him as the result of the enormous interest felt by the public all over the world by these scripts." The messages were published in book form in 1921. After their publication Vale Owen was persuaded by well-meaning friends to resign from his Living and take up touring and lecturing, and he visited America during this phase; but his rather shy and retiring personality, which, in conjunction with his unselfish devotion to duty, fitted him so well for his task as a parish priest, was ill-adapted to this new field, and, as soon as the original sensation had died down, Vale Owen found himself unsuccessful in his new work without being able to return to his old. His last years were passed in the grip of a painful malady and he died in 1931.

But although in the eyes of the world Vale Owen's life may appear to have ended in failure, I am confident that the results of his self-sacrificing work will eventually be recognized, and that he will be acknowledged as one who allowed no worldly considerations to deter him from his duty in transmitting to humanity messages of such vital importance to their spiritual welfare.

Now I do not for a moment maintain that because these messages came through a man of Vale Owen's character, they must necessarily be true; he was merely the receiver, and has no responsibility for their truth or falsity. If the messages are going to bring conviction to anyone, they must stand or fall on the essential merits of their probability, when taken in conjunction with other messages received from and through totally different sources. It is a matter of complete amazement to me that these messages, purporting to bring a revelation of such vital importance to the world, should have lapsed into comparative obscurity, especially after the sensation caused by their original appearance.

I think that possibly the basic reason for this is the apparent insipidity of the messages, taken as a whole—the lack of incident and exciting action. I find the objections very forcibly put in the only criticism of the Vale Owen books which happens to have come to my notice. Oddly enough it is written by a friend of my own, whose name I withhold on account of the hard things I have to say about his writings: for the same reason I withhold the name of his book. I quote him in *extenso* lest I be accused of taking anything out of its context, and because the point at issue is really of great importance. This is what he says: — "I shall try to be fair, and shall therefore make no play with passages merely because they lend themselves to humorous treatment, such as, for instance, the interesting information that Queen Victoria "is living in quite a small house. It is her wish." The book must be judged as a whole. A few grotesque incidents could easily be explained as mere glosses on a genuine text, the unconscious admixture of Vale-Owenism with an authentic spirit message. But it is not the glosses that worry me. It is the hopelessly unconvincing atmosphere of the script as a whole.

M. Andre Maurois has written a charming book called *Meipe*. Meipe is the land where all our dreams come true. The child's Meipe is a country where sweets are never forbidden, where grownups are sent to bed at tea-time, and where transport from place to place is effected by will-power and, if necessary, by wings.

Mr. Vale Owen's heaven is just Meipe and nothing more. It is the place where dreams come true.

"Aerial travel is the ordinary method adopted for long journeys.

This is usually effected by the effort of the will, without mechanical appliances. These are sometimes used to add variety, but are not necessary, and are employed for pleasure rather than for the business of the spheres." Meipe is, of course, a beautiful place.

"Visits are made to the dwellings of old friends. The newcomer is taken into magnificent forests where the trees form avenues like the aisles of some great Gothic cathedral. He views the flowers, some of them very large, of colours glorious in their purity. Some of these colours we have not on earth. He is shown the glorious semi-transparent temples, colleges, palaces of the rulers and other architectural beauties of the heavenly land. Mountains, rivers, lakes make up the panorama of the grand domain." Very like my own Meipe at the age of ten—especially the mountains.

Contrast flavours life, and existence would be insipid if our friends were all alike, and if they were all equally good, kind and helpful. It is a test of the good novel that the characters should be sharply differentiated—in one word, alive. You should not require the writer's signpost "Said Harry,"

"Paul tartly replied," etc., you should be able to recognize at once that it is Harry or Paul who is speaking. By this test Mr. Vale Owen fails, and it is at least a tribute to his honesty that his characterisation is so weak. You may read page after page of his book, and only discover by diligent research whether Ariel Zabdiel or Arnel is addressing you. All these spirit guides speak exactly the same language, drop the same platitudes, pour out the same unending stream of insipid sayings, tender, wise, grave and helpful, but unenlightened by the least gleam of humour, the least hint of a real live personality.

Let us accompany our spirit guides to the Celestial College and listen while the Principal of the College improves the shining hour.

"The Principal of the College was very courteous and kind, for all his high office. I suppose you would call him a great angel . .

He is very beautiful both of form and countenance; radiant and beaming and glowing would perhaps describe him best. He listened and encouraged us now and then with a quiet word, to state our difficulties, and we forgot that he was so high in estate, and talked without fear or restraint. And then he said "Well my dear pupils —for so you are good enough to become for a little time—what you have told me is very interesting ... (A great deal more of this sort of thing, and then in conclusion:) " 'Also you will be able to talk over with them the lessons I have been happy enough to be able to give you, and among you, you will, no doubt, have something more to tell and to ask me when we meet again a little later.' " All very nice and improving, but how dull. Very little of this sort of thing would make one long for the grumpiest of old dons, the most irritating of those schoolmasters who plagued one's youth, for anyone in short who had not lost all the infirmities of the flesh, and all trace of personality. What has happened to Jowett and Keats and Hornby and "O.B."? Surely the Celestial Powers can find some use for their talents among the Celestial Universities.

"Everything here seems to be of love and brightness," says one of Mr. Owen's spirit guides. Precisely. A great deal too much love and brightness. Real life owes its fascination to the contrast between brightness and gloom, to the clash of love and hate.

What are they doing with Cervantes and Swift, Rabelais and *Erewhon Butler*? Is there no irony, no humour, no wit in the life beyond? Let Ariel answer. Yes. It appears that they have their moments of glad mirth in the Lowlands of Heaven. He supplies us with a happy illustration. A group of spirits were trying to create a fruit tree by will power. They were not quite successful.

"The chief points of failure were that some of the fruit was ripe and some unripe. And the leaves were not correct in colour. Nor the branches right in proportion."

"And so we tried one thing after another, and found ourselves a little more successful each time. You can imagine something of the joy of such schooling as this, and the laughter and happy humour which resulted from our mistakes. Those among you who think that in this life we never make jokes, and never even laugh, will have to revise their ideas some day or they will find us strange company—or perhaps we shall find them so."

"Innocent fun no doubt, but a little lacking in the caustic flavour of earth-bound humour." Now all this is very much below my friend's usual standard of accuracy and honesty in criticism. In the first place he says that he will make no play with the interesting information about Queen Victoria; yet he plants his barbed dart for what it is worth. I have been unable to find any mention of Queen Victoria in the whole book.

Again, the passages which he quotes do not emanate from some high angel, but from Vale Owen's mother. My friend declaims "Let Ariel answer," and then quotes Mrs. Owen. I don't suppose that clergymen's mothers as a class are specially gifted with a sense of humour on earth. Mrs. Owen may have been so gifted, but my friend has no reason to assume that this was the case.

Nevertheless, the gravamen of the indictment is that Heaven lacks a sense of humour—that mordant humour of which my friend is so great an exponent, and of which the passage quoted is so admirable a sample. I must freely confess that I feel very much as my friend does on this subject.

If ever I get to Heaven I will give up my roast beef and my glass of port, I will give up my shooting and fishing, I will surrender my bank-balance (perforce), I will give up competitive games and the chief seats in the synagogue, the sinful lusts of the flesh shall pass unregretted—all these will I surrender, but how I shall hate to give up the exercise of my brand of humour. Yet I shall have to, because much of our humour is founded on cruelty or malice.

"Honour and wit foredamned they sit." The West African negro will roar with laughter at the sight of a dog with a broken leg, and, though we may have risen a little above that level, I thought that there was not so much difference when I saw the hilarity provoked by that revolting spectacle an All-in wrestling match on the sole occasion when I saw one. True, it was soon obvious that the contestants were Master Illusionists and were taking the greatest pains not to hurt one another in spite of their screams, roars, grunts and groans; but it was none the less a truly bestial display. Humour rises from the injury incurred by the man who slips on a banana skin and the humiliation of a man with a hole in his trousers, through the humour of dirt and the humour of blasphemy, to the bitter humour of the critic who scores his point and makes his victim squirm. True there is a certain type of humour which contains no element of malice, but I am sorry to say that a high proportion of our humour will fail to pass the mesh of the net of charity.

Is there an insurmountable barrier between the ordinary human intelligence and a conception of the joy of Heaven? Must we wait in a sort of melancholy hope that things will somehow be different when we die and that it will be "all right on the night?" I think we can do a little better than that.

I think we may start by dividing our earthly pleasures and joys into two classes, one of which may be expected to survive death, and the other not. We must obviously be prepared to jettison all those gratifications arising solely from success in the struggle for existence and the perpetuation of the race. These include, of course, the pleasures of the table, financial success through industry and gambling, and the attainment of a position of power in the community. They also include those pleasures deriving ultimately from the savage joy of killing one's enemy. In this category must be included the "manly sports" which train and toughen the young men of the country and the ridiculous competitive games in which so much of our adult energy is frittered away. Huntin', shootin' and fishin' also can have no rational appeal beyond the grave.

Then there are other pleasures, morally questionable, which may perhaps remain to be overcome in the afterlife. One of these is vainglory ("I got through Sphere Four in six months, and poor old Artemas has been there seven years"). There is also the deep mystery of sex, which will apparently persist beyond the grave although in a radically altered form.

On the other hand there are types of earthly pleasure which we can imagine as being retained and intensified manifold in the afterlife. Not least of these derive from the aesthetic sense. The messages indicate, and it is not unreasonable to suppose, that our capacity for enjoying beauty and colour will be widened both in range and intensity (there are constant references to "colours not visible to you"), and this may account for the eagerness with which spirits appear to flock to the various displays arranged for their benefit. After all, crowds used to brave difficulties of transport and assemble at the Crystal Palace to see the -Brock's Benefit displays of fireworks. If one admits the probability that much more beautiful displays may be staged in the afterlife, resulting in definitely pleasurable advances in spiritual experience, one can at least imagine that these spectacles may be eagerly looked forward to instead of being regarded as insipid or monotonous.

Again, the joy of Music is a closed book to many on earth. To such it may constitute a new source of happiness in the afterlife, and it may afford a new and intensified delight to those who were music lovers on earth.

Then, to me at any rate, the extension of knowledge is an intense satisfaction. The latest theories of wave-mechanics and atomic physics are of absorbing interest, although my limited brain capacity and my fragmentary education ill equip me to understand them. It would be pure pleasure to go to school again with a new model brain and satisfy all my perplexities; I don't think I should even yearn for a grumpy and irritating instructor. Next there is that deep human satisfaction "A man's sense of work well done and acknowledged by his peers." I think that this will rank high among the pleasures of the afterlife.

Lastly, there must be that supreme joy, afforded to giver and taker alike, by the exercise of unselfish love and charity. Personally I can but dimly conceive it and I imagine that my friend shares my difficulty; but there are saints on earth (alas too few) who feel already, even in this world, that this is their chief and pervading joy, for it is the peace of God which passeth all understanding.

And so perhaps, after all, to souls who will try to shed their earthly ideas with their earthly envelopes, Heaven may not prove to be such a monotonous and insipid place as we are apt to suppose.

At any rate, if one thing is more generally agreed than another in the messages which we are considering, it is that the soul which hugs its earthly notions to its breast will not get the chance of finding out until time or education shall have induced a new attitude of mind.

While we are on the subject I should like to deal rather more fully with my friend's investigations into Psychical Research and Spiritualism. Under the former heading he deals with physical manifestations such as ectoplasm, levitation, the production of music, the transportation of matter through matter, etc. Although he does not actually say so, it is quite obvious that he is personally convinced of the actuality of some of these phenomena, and he turns the hose of his irony on to the sceptic instead of the believer. He says: "Now the evidence for physical phenomena is very much stronger than the evidence for the Resurrection, and it is indeed quaintly inconsistent to accept the evidence for miracles which occurred nineteen hundred years ago before an uneducated and unscientific audience and to refuse to believe in similar occurrences carried through in recent years under the most rigid of test conditions." As I have already said, I do not regard this subject as a matter of very great importance, except in so far as it indicates a field of research which has been neglected by serious scientists.

Investigation might not only increase the sum of human knowledge, but might result in an improvement in the means of communication between this world and the next.

It is over his chapter on Spiritualism that I must break a lance with my friend. We must consider him as being something more than the Plain Blunt Man. He is a practised and influential controversialist with an active and inquiring mind. His writings carry conviction to the superficial reader, yet I think there is a basic confusion in the arguments adduced on this subject.

The trouble arises in his first sentence, which reads: *Spiritualism is the religion based on Psychical Research.* (My italics.) Now everyone is perfectly entitled to make his own definitions concerning the subject which he proposes to discuss, but this very narrow definition has, I think, led to some confusion of thought.

Supposing that I go to a medium and make contact with the spirit of my dead uncle, who tells me where the Missing Will is to be found. Is that Spiritualism? If not what else is it? Yet it has nothing to do with Religion.

If my friend insists on a religious connotation for the word "Spiritualism," he must provide us with another label for the general study of intercommunication with spirits. For, although again he does not say so, it seems quite clear that he is personally convinced of the reality of spirit communication. For instance, he writes: "Finally there are a very few well-authenticated cases in which the spirit control reveals knowledge of facts concerning the dead communicator, facts unknown to any living person, but which are none the less verifiable, and which have been verified. Neither thought reading nor telepathy can be evoked as a hypothesis to explain such cases, unless we assume that all memories and all emotions form a sort of cosmic pool which the medium can tap by a process that might be called deferred telepathy. But this explanation is even more improbable than the spiritualistic solution." Later on he quotes an instance where the location and dimensions of a buried chapel were revealed to excavators by means of automatic writing, and he is also impressed by the contents of the *Scripts of Cleophas* (already referred to) and the circumstances in which they were produced.

In spite of this my friend writes: "The main objection to the spiritualistic hypothesis is the marked degeneration of great men when they die, and the painful contrast between their living and their discarnate personalities.

"Discarnate intelligences rarely rise above the level of a low grade Moron. They seldom give a plain answer to a plain question, They throw no light on the problems of this life. No discovery in physics, chemistry or mathematics, no new idea in art or literature can be traced to our spirit guides." Now here he has definitely allowed his eloquence to run away with him. Moron is a nice round word, it flows trippingly from the pen, it means Fool in Greek, but it has nowadays a detestable connection with vicious idiocy. The statement is cruel and untrue.

It will give deep pain to some, and may deter others from the study of a subject which, whatever conclusions they may form, will at least tend to raise them from the level of crass materialism.

As regards giving a plain answer to a plain question, *Letters from the Other Side* attempts to do nothing else. If some of the answers are not very plain it is because the questions deal with deep mysteries. Philemon does his honest best.

In a later chapter I shall deal with the statement that no discoveries in science, or ideas in the arts, can be traced to spirit guides.

Later on, in order to account for the triviality of messages, my friend develops a theory that the medium "only succeeds in tapping dead men's dreams," and "merely succeeds in detaching from the subconscious mind of the dead a few trivial earth memories." Oddly enough, this same Philemon tells us quite definitely that this is true in some cases—he says: "but I know of the boys and men who slept here and in their dreams enjoyed banquets (they had starved on earth); and, remember, these dreams are often transmitted by mediums as well as the waking experiences of those who are here." This explanation probably accounts for a number of disjointed, illogical and fragmentary messages, but it cannot be taken seriously as a general explanation of spirit communication.

The fact is, of course, that some of the more serious and consecutive messages make a sustained attack on Christian doctrines as taught today. The impact of the Spiritualist Religion on our creeds and dogmas is terrific (if *Spirit Teachings* may be taken as the Spiritualists' Bible). Personally I do not accept this without protest, as will be seen from the last chapter of this book, but I think that if my friend had not started off by defining Spiritualism as a Religion we should have received a more dispassionate and logical article from his pen.

Spiritualism and Religion, though constantly overlapping, are essentially separate. But the statements which we receive through the agency of Spiritualism are bound to have a very disturbing effect on orthodox members of the Christian Churches. Hence the fervid opposition to Spiritualism shown by many otherwise open-minded people.

CHAPTER 8

THE SPHERES

Now to my main task! I want you to think of the Earth as the centre of a series of hollow spheres each bigger than the last. The first sphere practically corresponds to the earth's surface in location though not in substance, and the number of spheres in their outward order is indefinite so far as our knowledge goes; nothing higher than the fifteenth, however, is mentioned in Vale Owen's book. Each of these spheres represents a state of spiritual development a little in advance of that below, and the soul s progress is steadily onward and outward once the restrictions of earth are left behind.

These restrictions may be slight and soon surmounted, or they may be grievous and may take centuries (of our time) to overcome; but sooner or later every soul will be set onto the path of progress and light.

Now don't think of these spheres in too materialistic a way: they are real enough and solid enough to their inhabitants, and they have mountains and seas very much like those on earth, but they are quite invisible to us and cannot be perceived by any of our senses.

This is a hard saying, because we can see the sun and, beyond that, the stars; and we may say to ourselves that we know there cannot be anything but empty space between us and them. But in saying so much we are wrong, even by our own scientific standards.

It is a fact that there are layers at various heights above the earth which reflect wireless waves. One of them is called the "Heaviside Layer," and it is this which enables short-wave wireless to be effective over great ranges of earth. If it were not for the reflecting action of this layer, the signals would pass straight out into the infinite. It is interesting to know that Radio-Location was discovered during the investigation of these reflections by government scientists.

Fifty years ago our chemists and scientists thought that the smallest possible subdivision of matter was the atom, and that the atom was a small hard grain of solid substance, far too small to be seen by the most powerful microscope. Now they know that they were right about the existence of atoms, but wrong about their nature. Each atom is a little solar system of particles of positive and negative electricity in ceaseless motion, and when you ask them what electricity is, they cannot tell you.

So our "matter," for all that it looks and feels so solid, is nothing but a conglomeration of countless billions of electric particles in ceaseless and violent agitation in tiny orbits. It looks solid because it obstructs the passage of that particular band of etheric waves which affects our optic nerves and which we call Light, and it feels solid because the bouncing particles in matter repel the bouncing particles in our hands or in the soles of our boots. If our optic nerves had been constructed to react to X-rays and not to what we call Light, we should be able to see through matter suitably illuminated but we could not see the sun: and if our bodies were built up from electricity having the X-ray wavelength, we could pass through matter because the bouncing particles of matter would not resist the bouncing particles of our new and different bodies.

All this may seem to the scientist to be very childishly and ignorantly stated, and it may seem very great rubbish to the unscientific. But it contains the essence of the truth, which is that the laws of science operate in both worlds and there is nothing "supernatural." We call things supernatural only because we do not understand them. Anyway you have got to follow me in thinking of the next life as taking place in solid and substantial bodies in a solid and substantial world or we shall not get any further.

The next difficulty is that, if we think of a series of hollow concentric spheres, we can't get from one to the next without climbing through a hole in the roof or cutting a hole in the floor.

Well, things don't work out like that; "There is no void between any Spheres." I can't explain it and it is probably explicable only by a visualisation of Fourth Dimension mathematics which is beyond the capacity of our particular kind of brain; but I can give you a queer little instance of the unexpected effect of putting a "kink" into the three-dimensional space which we can understand.

Take a strip of paper about 12 inches long and
strip cut off the edge of a sheet of foolscap wil'
and hold the two ends together with your fingers.
metrical figure with two surfaces and two edges.

That is to say that a fly would have to cross an edge to get hٮ
face to another, and would have to cross a surface to get from edge ٮ
Now put a half-twist into the paper and join the ends with gum or stamֆ
paper. You have now got a figure with only one surface and one edge: that
is to say that the fly can reach any part of the surface without crawling over
an edge, and any part of the edge with crossing the surface.

Now guess what will happen if you get a pair of sharp-pointed scis-
sors and cut round the centre line of the ring. I won't spoil your fun by
telling you: try it and see.

I only mention this to induce a note of due humility towards celestial
geometry and mathematics, and to show you that our world is real and
solid to us only because we, and what we call matter, exist in a world
made up of particles of electricity jigging to a particular tune and ir-
radiated by a single octave of vibrations which we call Light.

There are other tunes and other octaves by the score in which "reality" lies elsewhere, and in which it is our world that is mist, and we
who are drifting ghosts. God is the great Mathematician and the great
Scientist. All things operate according to His laws, and our eyes will
be opened in His good time.

Now, as I dimly conceive it, each outward sphere operates on a new
wave-length, and a spirit in Sphere Ten would be just as invisible to
a spirit in Sphere Two as the spirit in Sphere Two would be to us, but
the spirit in Sphere Ten has the power of conditioning himself so as to
be visible and to operate in any lower Sphere, though the converse of
this is not true. If a spirit attempts to stray prematurely into a higher
Sphere, he is blinded and oppressed by the intensity of the unaccustomed light and so returns to his own place.

"His own place": that is the keynote of the future life. That is the secret of Judgment Day.

There are spirits who cannot bear even the dim radiance of Sphere
One. These go and consort with their like in lower regions and they
make for themselves their own Hell.

Later on I shall give some account of conditions there, and you will
see that there is no need for devils with pitch forks and lakes of burning brimstone. Man's inhumanity to man is quite sufficient, as we can
imagine from what we see on earth.

Even in a Nazi concentration camp the guards must have some humanity, the prisoners may help and cheer one another by unselfish thoughts and deeds, and kindly death comes as a release from the worst tortures. But imagine such a camp where all are all bad, warders and prisoners alike, and where death may not be wooed by any device. Add to these external torments an internal state of envy, hatred, malice and unsatisfied lusts—That is Hell.

Yet there is no personal Devil. Evil is not a positive thing in itself—it is merely the effect of obstruction to, and the negation of, Good. Every soul will eventually be set on the upward path, and even the great Archangels of Darkness will eventually come into the light.

The subject of Hell is not much dwelt on in the books which I have read, because their main object is to give encouragement to us on earth; but I shall later quote from a detailed description of a rescue visit to Hell, and Julia says: "The joy of Heaven is emptying Hell." Most of the books which I have read were communicated by spirits in a comparatively high stage of development and even Vale Owen's mother passed quickly through those spheres in closest contact with earth, but we have enough data to form a picture of the human soul in the early stages of its pilgrimage into the hereafter.

Starting with the moment of death, I think it is unnecessary to add very much to the vivid and graphic pictures given in Chapter 6 in so far as deaths on the battlefield are concerned. The thread which runs through them is the non-realization of the fact of death for the time being, and the instinctive desire to continue active fighting at first, merging into a desire to meet and help dead comrades when the fact of death is realized.

Private Dowding tries to help two of his pals to carry his own body down the trench labyrinth to a dressing station and says: "When I found that my pals could carry my body without my help, I dropped behind; I just followed in a curiously humble way. . . .

My body went to the first dressing station, and after examination was taken to a mortuary. I stayed near it all night, watching, but without thoughts. It was as if my being, feeling, and thinking had become 'suspended' by some Power outside myself. This sensation came over me gradually as the night advanced, I still expected to wake up in my body again—that is, so far as I expected anything.

Then I lost consciousness and slept soundly. . . . When I awoke my body had disappeared! How I hunted and hunted! It began to dawn upon me that something strange had happened, although I still felt I was in a dream and should soon awake. My body had been buried or burned, I never knew which. Soon I ceased hunting for it. Then the shock came! It came without any warning, suddenly. I had been killed by a German shell! I was dead! I was no longer alive! I had been killed, killed, killed. Curious that I felt no shock when I was first driven out of my body. Now the shock came, and it was very real. . . . How does it feel to be 'dead'? One can't explain because there is nothing in it! I simply felt free and light. My being seemed to have expanded." In Vale Owen's book another young soldier wakes up lying on the grass where he has been carried, and his first question is: "What about my kit please? Have I lost it?" Then he says: "But who brought me here? I don't remember this country. It was not like this when I was hit. Say, Sir, have I gone West?" Later: "Was it you, Sir, who came to me one night on sentry and spoke to me about going West?" He is told: "No, it is someone waiting for you a little further up the road." So they go on and he meets a comrade whose life he had tried to save a few days earlier.

In every case, every soul is met by some friend or messenger although the latter is not always visible to him. That is why Colonel Gascoigne asks us for our prayers. Through Mrs. Gascoigne he writes: "We who passed on before the war shook your plane to its foundations, ask over the ether for the help of you who are taking part in the earth life. We ask it in the name of those who die on the battlefields, on the sea, and in the air. We are guarding and protecting them in every way we can, but with your help we could do much more. We need your earth vibration, your personal affection, and the desire which you all have to lend a hand to those brave men who are protecting you, and whose lives are the price paid for your future upon earth." He also says sadly: "Prayer for us is lacking in your services on earth, as we are always left out or put aside, when we are so near to you—so near." The circumstances of an ordinary deathbed are more organized because there is opportunity for more careful preparation. Julia gives a detailed account of her own passing at the very beginning of her book and another later; and Vale Owen gives a description of the death of a woman in hospital similar in essentials. Often the spirit of a mother or grandmother comes to the bedside to greet a newly liberated soul. If loved relatives are not able to be present at the deathbed, the soul is generally led in a conscious or unconscious state to some spot where a meeting with dear ones takes place.

The newly liberated soul is often very sad to see the uncontrollable grief of those left behind, and to be unable to make them see or hear that there is nothing to weep about, but that all is well.

There appears to be an actual cord or cords connecting the soul with the body. The soul normally passes outside the body before death, and death occurs at the moment of the severance of the cord.

A scientific observation of the passing of a soul was recently made by the author of Private Dowding and is included in the last chapter of that book. When I say "scientific," I mean that exact methods of observation were employed, over a period of 76 hours, by one who would have seen nothing had he not been a medium.

The observations are followed by a message from the spirit himself giving his own impressions of his passing.

I do not reproduce the account here because, for one thing, it is a little grim, and, for another, I think that the case is rather unusual as regards the prolonged period spent by the spirit in apparent coma; but those interested may readily obtain the account for themselves, as the little book has just been reprinted and is amply worth getting for its other contents.

So far as I can understand, Sphere Two is the place to which newly arrived souls are first taken. "There is in the second Sphere from earth a house where those who are newly come over await their sorting-out, to be forwarded, each with his guide, to the place where he may best be trained in the beginnings of the heavenly life." This is possibly similar to that "Rest Hall" to which Private Dowding was taken; and Raymond. "I am here. ... I have seen that boy, Sir Oliver's son; he's better, and has had a splendid rest.

Tell his people." Here, in so far as there is an external Judgment at all, the Judgment takes place. But it is only a selection by spirit guides of the surroundings in which the soul will most probably find itself at ease; and the decision, if it errs at all, is most likely to err on the side of charity. The Judgment of the Soul is its own and comes from within. We sometimes say in this life "It's a free country," but we don't really mean it. We can't do or say what we want to, and we are scarcely allowed even to think honestly, especially in wartime; but over there it really is a free country, we can go where we like and find our own level. If the light is too bright we cannot bear it; and so we go each to his Own Place, and everyone is his own Judge. It makes you think a bit, doesn't it? Now of the awful mystery of Hell I shall say nothing at this moment, but I must give you what I can in description of Sphere One, which seems roughly to correspond with the Catholic state of Purgatory. To this region gravitate those who, though not desperately wicked, have led selfish and self-centred lives and who have laid up for themselves treasure (in the widest sense of the word) on earth. Vale Owen tells us little of this Sphere because his mother never merited a sojourn there, and the other communicators are high spirits who do not concern themselves much with this state of existence. To Julia's bright spirit no such experience was known; and Raymond went directly to the task of meeting and helping those killed on the battlefield (though perhaps his cigar-smoking friend may have taken a different path).

Private Dowding has given us a picture of his French editor friend: it finishes up: "Yes, I think the war is going on all right.

Our circulation has increased again, but alas! Guilbert cannot get enough paper. I wish I were down there. I would have laid in a big stock months ago." It is the "Living Dead Man" who is most communicative about that state, although he has such a different outlook from that of any of the other communicating spirits that it is wise to keep in mind that his experiences may be abnormal. (As I said, I shall later devote a special section to this astonishing book.) I told you about his friend who lived in a boarding house and complained of the coffee. Here are a few more extracts about the same lady.

"She said she was not having a very pleasant time. She found that everyone was interested in something else and did not want to talk with her."

"What do you talk to them about?"

"Why, I tell them my troubles as one friend tells another; but they do not seem to be interested. How selfish people are! ... I sometimes told myself that I would not be bothered with boarding house landladies and their careless hired girls; but they are just as bad here, even worse."

"Do you mean to tell me that you live in a boarding-house?"

"Where should I live? You know I am not rich."

"And what do you eat?"

"The same old things, meat and potatoes and pies and puddings...."

"What do you mean by 'out here'?"

"Why, before you died."

"But, man, I am not dead!" On another occasion he writes: "One day I met a lady recently arrived. She had not been here long enough to have lost her assurance of superiority over ordinary men and angels. That morning I had on my best Roman toga, for I had been reliving the past; and the lady, mistaking me for Caesar or some other ancient aristocrat, asked me to direct her to a place where gentlewomen congregated. I was forced to admit that I did not know of any such resort. She glanced at my classical garment.

"Perhaps you are an actor," she said.

"We are all actors here," I replied. "We have acquired the tolerance and courtesy of children who never ridicule one another's play."

"Is heaven merely a play-room?" she asked, in a shocked tone.

"Not at all," I answered, "but you are not in heaven." Her look of apprehension caused me immediately to add "Nor are you in hell, either." Again he writes: "One day I met a man in doublet and hose who announced that he was Shakespeare. Now I have become accustomed to such announcements, and they do not surprise me as they did six or eight months ago, . . . This playing of a part is quite innocent, though sometimes the very ease with which it is done brings with it the temptation to deception, especially when dealing with the earth people. You will see the point I wish to make. The 'lying spirits' or which the frequenters of séance rooms so often make complaint, are those astral actors, who may even come to take a certain pride in the cleverness of their art. Be not too sure that the spirit who claims to be your deceased grandfather is that estimable old man himself. He may be merely an actor, playing a part for his own entertainment and yours." You must bear in mind that the "Living Dead Man" views these souls with a good-humoured tolerance, because he is himself bound to earth (as he thinks) indefinitely, and has no wish to break away.

Their state is not regarded with such equanimity by higher and less self-centred spirits. Zabdiel, for instance, says: "Those who are held to be in the world, therefore, are spiritually in the sphere which is near the earth; and these are sometimes called earth-bound spirits. It matters not whether they be clothed with material bodies, or have shed them and stand discarnate; these are bound and chained to the world, and cannot rise into the spheres of light, but have their conversation among those who move in the dim regions about the planet's surface. These are holden of the earth, and are actually within the circumference of the earth's sphere." And in another place: "These three spheres nearest the earth were treated more or less as one region, for here the vapour of earth's hell-soup was thick about us." Sphere Three seems to be the highest of these directly associated with earth. This would be the habitat of spirits like Raymond and Private Dowding, and the workers under Colonel Gascoigne who are designated for further advancement but retained for the time being on the duty of meeting soldiers killed in battle and other work bringing them directly in touch with earth.

It also appears to be the site of Universities or Halls of Instruction, as Private Dowding calls them. He gives an account of one. The teaching is done through signs and symbols, pictures, rays and cinema effects. A lesson in the control of the emotions is described. The teacher shows in a crystal globe the mind of a man still on earth—a successful and ambitious merchant. "If peace is signed soon I will visit New York and open a branch there; that will come in useful when Jack comes into the business; lucky he was too young to fight; wish the school bills were not so heavy; shall cut out the University now; wish I had a second boy, too many girls; it can't be helped now; must try to get them married soon; what was that Ada told me this morning about young Mr. Morgan? Wonder what his father's worth? I might find out, used to be on Change, but the war may have broken him; Johnson may know, Johnson hasn't paid that bill, must ring him up; etc., etc." Private Dowding comments: "His was not a vicious mind, simply uncontrolled, self-centred, unilluminated. It was shown to us as a common type." Vale Owen's mother describes for us various other Universities at the same, or a slightly more advanced, level of instruction.

Descriptions are given of a College of Music, Halls of Colour, a Hall showing Earth's physical history and evolution, and a Hall of Chemistry. Here are some extracts from an account of a visit to the Hall of Evolution: "In the centre was a large structure, and this we entered and found ourselves in a large and spacious hall, the only compartment in the place. It was circular in shape, and round the walls were carvings of a curious kind. We examined them and found that they were representations of the heavenly bodies; and one was the earth. But they were not fixed, but turned on pivots, half in and half out of the wall. There were also models of animals and trees and human beings, but they were all movable, and stood on pedestals in niches or alcoves. We inquired the meaning and were told that this was a purely scientific institution.

"We were taken up to a balcony on one side of the circular space. It projected somewhat, and so we could see the whole at once.

Then we were told that a small demonstration would be made for our benefit in order that we might get some idea of the use to which these things were put.

"At length a blue mist began to fill the central space. Then a ray of light swept round the hall and rested on the globe which represented the earth. As it hovered about it the sphere appeared to absorb the ray and became luminous, and after a time, the ray being withdrawn, we saw the earth globe was shining as from within.

Then another ray was sent on to it of a deeper and different kind, and the globe slowly left the pedestal, or pivot, or whatever it rested on, and began to float out from the wall.

"As it approached the centre of the space it entered the blue mist and immediately on contact began to enlarge until it became a great sphere glowing with its own light and floating in the blue space. It was exceedingly beautiful. Slowly, very slowly, it revolved on its own axis, evidently, in the same way the earth does, and we were able to see the oceans and continents. These were flat patterns, like those on the terrestrial globes used on earth. But as it revolved they began to assume a different aspect.

"The mountains and hills began to stand out, and the waters to sway and ripple: and presently we saw minute models of the cities, and even details of the buildings. And still more detailed grew the model of the earth, till we could see the people themselves, first the crowds and then the individuals. This will be hard for you to understand, that on a globe of some perhaps eighty or a hundred feet in diameter we were able to see individual men and animals.

But that is part of the science of this institution—the enabling of these details being seen individually.

"Still more distinct grew these wonderful scenes, and, as the globe revolved, we saw men hurrying about the cities and working in the fields. We saw the wide spaces of prairie and desert and forest and little animals roaming in them. And as the globe slowly circled we saw the oceans and seas, some placid and the others tossing and roaring, and here and there a ship. And all the life of earth passed before our eyes. . . . Soon the scenes began to change on the revolving sphere, and we were taken back through the thousands of years of the life of the earth and the generations of men and animals and plant life which had been from the present to the ages when men were just emerging from the forest to settle in colonies on the plains. . . . When we had satisfied our eyes for a while, the globe gradually became smaller and smaller and floated back to the niche in the wall, and then the light faded out from it and it looked like an alabaster carving, just as we had seen it at first set there as an ornament. . . . The animals about the walls were also used for a like purpose. One would be vivified by these powerful rays and brought into the centre of the hall. When so treated it could walk of itself like a live animal, which it was temporarily and in a certain restricted way. When it had ascended a platform in the centre space, then it was treated with the enlarging rays—as I may call them, not knowing their scientific name—and then with others which rendered it transparent, and all the internal organism of the animal became plainly visible to the students assembled.

"Then it was possible to bring over the living model a change, so that it began to evolve backward—or should I say 'involve'?— towards its simpler and primal state as a mammal, and so on. The whole structural history of the animal was shown in that life-like process. . . . Also it was possible for any student to take charge and continue the development according to his own idea, and this not of the animals alone, but of the heavenly bodies, and also of nations and peoples, which are dealt with in another hall, however, specially adapted to that study." Sphere Five is a difficult one to pass: "It is a critical sphere where attunement has to be made in a man's various traits and all inharmony done away." It is also the parting of the ways, where is chosen the future part of the spirit. "it is a kind of sorting room, as one should say, wherein are the inhabitants, in the course of their sojourn there, classified into their proper groups, and proceed onwards in that special branch of service for which they most properly are fitted." Sphere Ten is also of exceptional importance because it is the highest of those from which visitors commonly come down to earth level and below. After this stage it seems that some change occurs which makes visitations and communication with lower spheres more difficult. It is true that Manifestations of the Christ in Presence Form often occur in the lower spheres, and occasionally some great angel may descend for a special purpose, but, broadly speaking, it seems that Sphere Ten represents the limit of human comprehension as to its conditions. Beyond Sphere Ten, as I understand, human words are inadequate to give the remotest conception of spiritual life.

Sphere Ten has also another importance, because it is here that (sometimes at any rate) the followers of Non-Christian religions join up with the great river of spirit progress.

An account is given of the arrival of a party of Persian Fire worshippers from Sphere Nine, and their final relinquishment, as useless, of an Altar which they had cherished since their time on earth. Their leader says: "For we have, by much teaching on the part of others, and our own meditation, come to know that all God's children are of one birth and race, as children of the one Father alone. The time is now when it helps us no more to remember aught which divides, even though it be in love and general tolerance." The highest-numbered Sphere where conditions are at all known is the Fourteenth, and somewhere beyond this is the "Christ Sphere." There is one rather interesting circumstance which I have not mentioned in connection with the Spheres and that is that as the Spheres extend outwards through space, they more and more interpenetrate, and are affected by, similar Spheres centred on other heavenly bodies. (You can see this for yourselves if you get a plan of the Solar System and draw a number of concentric rings round the Sun and each of the planets.) Because of this it is indicated in Vale Owen's book that the old science of Astrology is not so dead as is generally believed: I say the Science of Astrology, and not the puerile superstition recently revived by some newspapers to the effect that all persons born between March 3rd and April 7th will find next Thursday afternoon a bad time to make investments.

I feel that, in an endeavour to give a matter-of-fact picture of the hereafter, I have laid insufficient stress on the constantly reiterated burden of the messages. These things, these sights, sounds, colours, landscapes, buildings, spirit-forms and raiment are unimaginably lovely to the senses. But I suppose that even if I had a magic pen, truly to describe all these marvels and glories, nobody on earth would be able to visualize the picture or to capture the atmosphere.

CHAPTER 9

THE HELLS

I n writing of the hells I have to rely almost entirely on Vale Owen's book, with only a few illuminating side-lights from other sources.

I propose to give an account of a rescue expedition led by an angel called Arnel. Arnel was an Englishman who taught music and painting in Florence during the Renaissance, and contributed most of the contents of the latter half of Vale Owen's book. I will give his account in abbreviated narrative form with fairly long verbatim extracts, so that you may get the atmosphere of his story.

Arnel with fourteen companions started from Sphere Ten and, after halts in Spheres Five and Three in order to condition themselves gradually to the changing spiritual atmosphere, they arrived in "that tract where people come on leaving earth, and of which we have already spoken in brief, and passed on into the darker realms." The geography of that part of the border land between Heaven and Hell which is dealt with in The Life Beyond the Veil is described as follows: "There is a region which is still in the sunlight, but ends in a steep descent, where the bottom lies in darkness.

As we stood there to view, we looked across the deep valley, which seemed to be filled with gloom so gross that we could not penetrate it from our standpoint in the light. Above the murky ocean of mist and vapour a dull light rested from above, but could not sink beneath the surface far, that ocean was so dense. And down into that we had to go.

"The Bridge of which your mother spoke to you runs right across the valley and lands on a lower elevation beyond. Those who from the depth climb up that side then rest a period at the further end, and come across the great causeway to the hither side.

There are rest houses here and there along the way where they who are too weary still to make the journey at one stage may stay and refresh themselves from time to time. For even after gaining the Bridge, the journey across is a painful one, inasmuch as on its either side they see the murk and gloom from which they have lately come, and hear the cries of those, their sometime companions, who still linger beneath, way down, in the valley of death and despair." This Bridge is apparently not the only way across the Borderland between Heaven and Hell. Julia speaks of another region as follows: "The Borderland which divides the two is crossed by innumerable paths by which the dwellers in Heaven are perpetually leading those who were spirits in prison." And Private Dowding crossed no bridge during his brief and abortive journey into Hell. Arnel continues: "So we took the path downwards, and as we went the gloom became more gloomy and the chill more full of fear. But we knew we went to help, and not to fear aught, and so we did not hesitate in our steps, but went warily withal, and looking this way and that for the right path, for our first station lay a little to the right hand as we went, and not between the Rest-land and the Ridge, and it was a colony of those who were weary of the deathlife they had endured, and yet who lacked the strength to break away, or the knowledge which way to take, if they should leave their present desperate anchorage. As we went, our eyes became more attuned to the gloom, and we could see about us, as on a night one might see the country outlying a city by the ruddy flares on the watchtowers thereof. We saw that there were many ruined buildings, some in clusters and some solitary. Decay was all about us.

It seemed to us that no one had even made whole any house, once it had begun to fall into disrepair. Having built it, they left it to build another elsewhere at the first sign of wear, or, having tired of it before it was finished, had left to build another. Listlessness and want of endurance was all about us in the air—the listlessness of weary despair and the despondency of doubt, both of their own strength and of their neighbours' purpose.

"There were trees also, some very large, but mostly leafless, and those with leaves not comely, for the leaves were of dark green and yellow, and spiked with lance-like teeth, as if they too took on the aspect of enmity from those who had lived near them. Here and there we crossed a waterway full of boulders and sharp stones and with little water, and that water thick with slime and stinking.

"And at long, long last we came within sight of the colony we were seeking. It was not a city, but a cluster of houses, some large and some small. They were scattered about, here and there, and not in order. There were no streets in the city. Many dwellings were merely mud huts, or a couple of slabs of stone to form a shelter.

And there were fires about the open spaces to give light to the inhabitants. Round these, many groups were gathered, some sitting in silence looking at the flames, others loudly brawling, others wrestling in their anger, one with another. So we drew near, and finding a silent group, we stood by waiting and looking upon these with much pitifulness in our hearts for their hopelessness of spirit.

And, seeing them, we took hands one of another and thanked our Father that He had given us this present work to do." Arnel finds the leader of the group; "a tall gaunt figure with knotted joints and limbs, bent and bowed, and his face was pitiful to see, such lack of hope and fullness of despair was there upon him." He recognized him as a magistrate whom he had known in earth life, and tries to touch him by mention of his wife. He says: "Yes I remember, and what of her? Do you bring news of her? Why did she leave me thus?" Arnel explains that she is in a higher sphere and cannot come to him until he has begun his upward journey. "He broke in upon me: 'Then she will not come to me now I have fallen upon evil times.' 'She cannot come all the way,' I said. 'You must go your way to her and she will meet you.' And at that he cried out in anger, 'Then let her be damned for a proud and hard-cased wench.

She was ever the fine lady-saint to me and moaning over my little lapses. Tell her, if you come from her parts, that she can stay in her spotless mansion and gloat upon her husband's state. They be here in plenty more pleasurable than she, if not so comely. And if she will descend from her high estate we will have a rousing rout for her reception. So good day to you, sir.' And sneering, he turned away and laughed to the crowd for their approval.

"But there arose one other of them who came and took him aside. This one had been sitting among them, and was drab of dress as any of them. Yet there was a gentleness in his movements and somewhat of grace withal which was to us surprising. He spoke to him awhile, and then they came back to me, and this companion said: 'Sir, this man did not quite understand the purport of your words, nor that you did really come to comfort and not to taunt.

He is some little repentant that he spoke to you in words such as were unseemly. I have told him that you and he were not altogether unknown to each other once. Of your kindness, sir, speak to him again, but not of his wife, for as yet he cannot endure her desertion, as he names her absence.' I was very much surprised at this speech, so quietly uttered, while the brawling noises came from all around us and shrieks and curses intermingled from the groups by the fires upon the plain. I felt that my business was with him in chief, for I had a sure conviction that could I impress him we would through him be able to concern his companions in their future course, for he seemed to be dominant among them and of consequence." Arnel succeeds in impressing the magistrate to some extent; then he seeks out the mediator "who seemed to me to be ripe for his journey out of that region into one more in tune with his repentant mind. I found him sitting apart on the bole of a fallen tree.

"Seeing me approach he stood and came towards me, and I said: 'My friend I thank you for your good offices, for I have, through your timely help, been able to impress that unhappy man as otherwise I had not done. You be more familiar with the natures of these your companions than I, and have used your experience to good effect. And now, what of your own life and future?' " 'I thank you, sir, in turn,' he replied. I ought no longer to delay the discovery of myself to you. I am not of this region, sir, but of the Fourth Sphere, and I am here by choice to do service, such as I am able, among these poor darkened souls.' 'Do you live here constant?' I inquired of him, amazed; and he replied: 'For a long time, yes. But when depression becomes too heavy, I return for a little while for replenishing to my own home and then come hither once again.' 'How often?' I asked him. 'Since I came here first,' he said, 'some sixty years have gone in earth-time, and I have returned to my home nine times. Several of those I knew on earth came here in the first early period, but none of late; they be all strangers now. Yet I still continue to help them one by one.' "At this I marvelled greatly and ashamed.

"Here my party came on tour and thought it a virtue so to do.

But the one who stood before me brought to my mind Another, who laid His glory aside and emptied Himself that others might be filled. I think I did not realize in fullness till then what it meant that a man should lay down his life for his friends, aye, and those friends such as these, and to dwell with them in these regions of the shadow of death. He saw me and understood some of what passed through my mind, and taking my own shame upon himself, he said wistfully; 'So much He did for me Sir—so much—and at so great a cost.' "And I said to him, taking his hand in mine; 'My brother, you have read me a lection of the very Book of God His Love. The Christ of God is beyond our understanding in the Majesty of His Beauty and His Love so wide and sweet. Him we may not comprehend, but only worship with adoration. But since this be so, it is something of profit to consort with one who knows how to attain to be a lesser Christ. And such, methinks, I have found in you.' "But he only lowered his fair head, and as I, of reverence led, kissed him where the parting of his hair was, murmured as to himself: 'If I were worthy—if only I were worthy of that Name.'" Thereafter the Party penetrates deeper into the regions of gloom: "As we went we felt about us a growing power of evil For you must mark there are degrees of Power, as of evil, in the different colonies there, and also diverse notes of evil dominant in its several regions. And, further, the inequality of forcefulness obtains there as in earth. They are not all of one type and pattern in evil. For free-will and personality are there, as elsewhere, and, by the persistence of these, some be great ones and some of less account in power, even as in earth and in the brighter spheres.

"Thus we came to a large city, and entered through a massive gateway, where guards marched to and fro. We had relaxed our will to visibility and so passed in unseen. We found the broad street beyond the gate was lined with great houses of heavy build like prison fortresses. From several of the wind-holes lurid flickering of light fell into the roadway and across our path. We went on until we came to a large square, where there was set up a statue on a high pedestal, not in the middle, but toward one side, where the largest building stood.

"The statue was that of a man who wore the toga of a Roman noble, and in his left hand he held a mirror, into which he looked, but his right hand held a flagon, out of which he poured red wine which splashed into the basin below—a travesty of nobility. The basin was ornamented with figures here and there around its border.

There were children at play, but the game they played was the torture of a lamb by flaying it alive. At another part there was a rudely carved woman, who held a babe inverted to her breast. The carvings were of such like nature, all of mockery, blaspheming the virtues of childhood, maternity, valour, worship, love and other, an obscene and motley crowd which made us near despair of good result by any appeal to nobility of those who lived in that city, Filth and mockery were rife all around us. Even the buildings ill their plan and ornamentation shocked the eye whichever way we turned. But we were there for a purpose, as I say, and we must stomach what we met, and go forward on our errand." The members of the party make themselves visible and pass into the Palace of Evil opposite the statue. Arnel continues: "Opposite! us there rose a great flight of steps from floor to balcony. All the crowd which filled the hall sat around and faced it. Upon the lower steps and half way up there were coiled, in different attitudes, all unbeautiful, men and women in loose and scanty clothing, which, nevertheless, made pretence to grandeur. Here and there a gold or silver belt, or chaplet, or silver brooch of jewels, or bejewelled buckle or clasp appeared; but all were false, as one could see: the gold was tinsel and the gems were counterfeit. Upon the stain, just above them, stood the speaker. He was of giant stature, bigger than them all, as he also dominated them in his wickedness. He wore a spiked crown and a long mantle of dirty grey, as if it once had been white but lacked the lustre of whiteness, and had taken on its neutral tone from the wearer. About his breast was a double girdle of false gold, which crossed and was gathered at each hip by a belt of leather. Sandals were upon his feet, and lying on the steps beside him a shepherd's crook. But what sent through our company, as we watched him, a pang of unutterable pain was the crown.

The spikes were the thorns of a bramble done in gold, which, circling his dusky brow, was wrought into a crown." The speaker preaches a blasphemous sermon, rather puerile, but I suppose it is quite difficult to be intelligently blasphemous when you come to think of it. He calls on his audience to follow him in a raid of evil spirits on to the earth.

To quote Arnel again: "He who assumed so gentle a character, and with so ill a grace, was one of the fiercest and most cruel despots of all that region. Truly, as he said, they had elected him Governor, but that was in fear of his great power of evil. And now that he called those poor misshapen, half-frenzied men noble, they applauded him in their servility for the self-same epaulette shone fair upon her brow as it bound her gold-brown hair, and the jewel of order upon her shoulder shone bright and true of her own virtue. About her middle was a belt of silver. And all these showed in relief against those tawdry jewels of the crowd before her. And in her arms she held a bundle of white lilies. She stood there, the presentiment of pure womanhood in all its perfect loveliness, a challenge to the late speaker's ribald cynicism of her race.

Then, when a long time they had looked upon her, both the men and the women there, one of them sobbed and tried to smother the sound in her mantle. But then the others gave way before the returning upon them of their sometime womanhood, and the hall was filled with the wailing of the women—oh, so hopeless to hear in that place of misery and of bondage, that the men also began to cover their faces with their hands, to sink upon the ground, and to press their foreheads in the thick dust upon the floor.

"But now the Governor took himself in hand, for he saw his power at hazard. He began to stride in great anger over the bodies of the women to get at her who first had set the pace of their weeping. But now I came down to the lowest step and called to him: 'Stay your hand and come hither to me.' "At this he turned and leered at me and began to say: 'But you, my lord, are welcome, so you come in peace among us. Yet these poor cravens be too much bedazzled of the light of that fair lady behind you, and I do but seek to bring them to their reason, so they shall give you proper welcome'.

"But I said very sternly to him: 'Cease and come hither.' So he came and stood before me, and I continued: 'You have taken upon you to blaspheme, both in speech and also by your trappings.

Take off that crown of blasphemy and lay down the shepherd's crook, you who dare to mock at One Who claims these His children whom you hold in your bond of fear.' These things he did, and then I spoke to some men standing near, and I said to them more gently: 'You have been cowards too long, and this man has enslaved you body and soul. He shall be taken to a city where one stronger in evil might than he rules. Do you, who have served him hereto, do now my bidding. Disrobe him of that mantle and that girdle which he has donned in his mockery of Him Whom even he shall own some day his Sovereign Prince and Lord."

"And then I waited, and there came forward four of them and began to unbuckle his belt. He turned in fierce rage upon them, but I had taken the staff from him, and this I laid upon his shoulder, and at the touch he sensed the power within me and strove no more. So my will with him was done; and then I bade him go forth of the hall into the darkness without, where guards awaited him to take him into that far region where as he had done to others it should be done to him." Then one of Arnel's party began to sing to the crowd now released from the fear of their Governor, and the party stayed for some time teaching and helping them. Later they were relieved by another party which stayed with those of the crowd who wished to escape, until they were ready to begin their journey towards the light.

Later, Vale Owen asks who were the guards that took the Governor away; and receives the following answer: "Ah, there you touch upon one of the difficult matters to understand until you learn more of the ways of God His Wisdom, and His Sovereignty.

In brief, know you, friend, that God is Sovereign not in Heaven alone but in Hell also, and in all the Hells He rules and He alone.

The others dominate locally, but He rules over them all. The guards I spoke of were men of that same city to which we sent the man. Evil men they were and did not own allegiance to the Creator of them all. But knowing not whose judgment delivered this one more victim into their hands, nor knowing it was for his ultimate salvation, they did our will without ado. You may find the key here, if you go beneath and deep enough, to much of that which happens on your earth.

"Evil men by many are thought to be outside the pale of His Kingdom; and evils and disasters to be faulty manifestations of His dynamic energising. But both are in His hand to use, and even evil men, unwitting, are made to work out His plans and purpose in the ultimate." After some further moralising on the use of evil men as the agents of ultimate good, Arnel continues: "And now, if you will, we would go forward with our narrative to tell you of some of the places we happened on, and what we did by them. As we went about we found many of those settlements where people of like mind sought to consort together. It was sad to see them who wandered from town to town in search of that companionship which should ease their loneliness, and finding shortly that agreement one with another was not to be had in any enduring measure, would wander again into the deserts to get away from those whom they had thought to offer some chance of ease and pleasurable company.

"We found that in nearly every colony there was one mastermind— and here and there more than one nearly equal in forcefulness of character—who dominated the rest, and enslaved them by the dread he sent forth upon them. Here is one whose city we came to once after a long journey through very desolate and forsaken country. The city itself was built about by a strong wall, and it was large in area. We went within and were challenged by the guard at the gateway." The Captain of the guard tries to arrest them but is overcome by a display of spiritual power and induced to lead the party to the mines, where thousands of souls are enslaved.

They came to a large cave-mouth which led into the bowels of the earth, and "There came forth in gusts a wind of odour so foul and hot and fetid that we drew back and paused awhile to call for strength." On the downward way the Captain was oppressed in spirit and his face was agonised and grey. Arnel continues: "So I said to him: 'Why are you become so sad, my guide? You have put on a sorry aspect since you drew near the mouth of these mines.' " 'Sir,' he answered and meekly now, 'I was once of those who work with pick and spade within these hell-furnaces, and the fear of it comes upon me now.' " 'Then search into your inmost soul for a grain of pity for those who work there now where once you suffered so sorely.' "He sank upon a boulder by the side of the path, overcome by weakness, and replied to my words with stranger words of his own: 'Nay, nay, 'tis needful I be pitied by them, not they by me.

Their lot is here, but mine is hell ten times doubled.' " 'How? Since you have escaped their slavery and come forth of the mines into a better state or service to the one you call your Lord?' 'I thought you were someone great in wisdom,' he replied with a bitter smile, 'and yet you do not understand that to fly from one state of servitude to another of higher degree in authority is to put off a hair shirt for one with thorns and brambles for web and woof.' "Then I took shame to myself that I had but just learned that lesson on top of others gathered of our experience in those dark tracts of hell." There follows a long description of the mines and the party descends into deeper and deeper workings: "Figures went hither and thither with furtive tread as if afraid some horror should start up in their pathway when they were most unaware. Now and then the clanging of chains came up to us, then a weird cry of agony and often a mad, wild laugh and the sound of a whip. All was sad both to hear and to see. Cruelty seemed to float in the air as one sufferer gave vent to his agony by torturing another more helpless." Arnel then tells the Captain to open all the gates separating one part of the mine from another. The Captain replies: "Sir, it is in my heart to do this; but I fear my lord the Chief. He is terrible in his wrath, sir, and even now I have a dread upon me, lest some spying hound should have sought to curry favour with him by carrying to him a report of what has already been done." But finally the Captain consents to give the order for the opening of the gates.

"Then in concert we lifted up our voices and sent forth a loud chorus of praise. It swelled louder and louder as we sang, and it filled all that place with its melody and penetrated the tunnel and filled the galleries

83

and the caves where the poor hopeless ones were doing good service to their lord, this cruel Prince of the Darkness, who held them bound by the fierceness of his evil strength. . . .

And as we sang, one after another of those slaves of evil came within sight of us. A pale grey face would half emerge from one tunnel and then from another, or from a cleft in the rock, and from holes and dens we had not noticed they looked forth upon us, until the whole of the cliffs around us were full of frightened, yet longing people, too timorous to come forth, yet gulping down the draught of refreshment like thirsty men in a desert. But others there were who looked forth in anger with red, shining eyes, which flashed their inner fires upon us, and others still who bowed their heads aground in their misery of remorse for past wrong-doing and for the memory of that mother's lullaby of which we had sung, and the way it had pointed and which they had spurned, and gone the other road—to this.

"Then we grew slowly softer, and ended in a sweet, long chord of rest and peace, and one long-drawn solemn 'Amen.' "Then one came forth and stood a little distance away from us and knelt and said 'Amen.' When the others saw this they drew in their breath to see what plague would strike him, for this was treason to the lord of the place. But I went forward and took him among us, and we closed him round, so none could do him harm.

Then they came forth to the number of four hundred, in twos and threes and then in dozens, and stood like children saying a lection, and murmured, as they had heard him do 'Amen, Amen.' And the while, those who stood or crouched still in the shadows of the galleries and of the boulders and crags hissed curses at us and them, but none came forth to try their tilt with us." Arnel addresses those remaining and warns them to school themselves so that they may be ready to come forth when the next expedition of rescue shall arrive.

Then there is a great commotion, and the Chief, who has heard of the intrusion, arrives on the scene. Here is Arnel's description of him: — "He was of stature gigantic, as tall as a man and half a man in height. His shoulders were unequal, his left lower than the right, and his head, nearly hairless, was thrust forward on a thick neck.

A tunic of rusty gold and sleeveless was upon him, and a sword hung on his left side from a leather belt which passed over his right shoulder. Rusty iron greaves he wore, and shoes of untanned skin, and on his brow a chaplet of silver, tarnished and stained, and on the front of it a boss carved into the semblance of some animal which might be

84

called a land-octopus, if such there were, symbolic of his evil power. His whole aspect was that of mock-royalty, or, more nearly, the striving after a royalty beyond his attaining. Evil passion, frenzy, lust, cruelty and hatred seemed to suffuse his dark face and to permeate his whole personality. And yet these overlaid potential nobility, and nullified what might have been great power for good, now turned to evil. He was an Archangel damned, and that is another way of saying 'arch-fiend'." Do you know what he had been in earth-life? "Your questions, friend, I like to answer, and when you ask them I cannot but feel some prompting leads you to do so which must have respect of me. And, therefore, I answer them. Do not cease to ask them, no, for there may be in them reason I do not reckon with and which I could find only by inquiry. But you will not mistake my meaning. If he was a great surgeon in a large hospital for the poor in your England, that does not predicate that others are as he. Had he been a priest or a philanthropist, it had been no more strange. For the outward seeming is not ever in consonance with the real man. Well, such he was, and there you have it in a word." The Captain meanwhile has been caught and bound: "This seeing, I at once stepped forward very quickly, and, as I went by the Chief, I touched the blade of his sword in passing, and then stood before those who held the bound man and commanded them: 'Loose that man of his thongs and set him forward towards our company."

"At these words a yell of rage broke from the Chief and he tried to raise his sword upon me. But all the temper had left the blade, and it hung down limp as water-weed, he staring in horror at it the while, for he took it at once as a token of his authority bereft of power. I had not in mind to make him a stock of laughter, but the others, his slaves, saw the comic element in his plight, not of humour but of malice, and from hidden places there came gusts of laughter and mockery. Then the blade withered and fell from the haft all rotten, and the haft he hurled at a point up among the rocks where someone laughed longer than his fellows." The Chief ostensibly submits to superior power and leads the way out of the mines to his palace. "As we had come through the mines, our company had been increased in length by those who had joined us from the caves which stretched into the darkness far away on either hand. News, so scarce among them, had been carried quickly to the farthest limits of these gloomy regions, and now our numbers were in thousands, where they had been hundreds before." They pass out of the cave-mouth and come into the open space among the huts of the workers. Here the liberated slaves are told to go through the city and spread the news of the rescue to such others as wish to join. The Chief leads the party of angels to his own house, where he asks them to wait in a room, and furtively locks the door while he gathers his army to recapture the slaves and his court to witness the discomfiture of the angels.

"We knew what we should do without counsel or discourse, so we took hands one of another and lifted ourselves towards the light and life of our own environment. As we aspired together, our condition gradually changed, and our bodies took on a nature more sublimate, so we passed hence without those walls, and stood in the square before the Principal Gate, awaiting the coming of our company.

"We did not see the Chief again. He had, as we knew, planned the recapture of those we had forced from his servitude, and even now these were being gathered from the regions about the city by runners sent forth, a great army, which was closing in on all sides to do vengeance on those who had made bold to flout his authority.

But I have naught dramatic to tell you, my friend—no clash of arms, no cries for mercy and no coming of an army of bright warriors to the rescue. It all fell out very tame and flat. In this wise: In that mock Throne Room he gathered his court, and, having torches lighted and placed all round the walls, and fires kindled all along the centre of the floor to light the hall, he made a great speech to his dusky retainers. Then the door of our anteroom was solemnly unbolted, and we were bidden come forth that he should do us honour. And when we were not found within, and his vengeance was thus denied to him, and his shame before his nobles manifest, and all come about by his own plans and actions, he broke down utterly, while they laughed to see him so in his abasement. Cruel jests they passed among them as they strolled away and left him alone, seated upon his stone chair aloft on the dais, defeated.

"Mark you, friend, how in these rebel states tragedy and gross buffoonery jostle one the other wherever you shall go. All is empty make-believe, for all is in opposition to the only Reality.

So these mock rulers are served by their people in mock humility, and are surrounded by mock-courtiers whose adulation is thrust through and through with stings and arrows of cynicism and ribald mockery." Here, unfortunately, the original script of one sitting has been lost; but all the souls rescued in the course of the expedition are placed under the care of "The lesser Christ" and the Captain, in a new colony where they may progress together towards the light.

This colony is referred to again on more than one occasion, and Arnel asks us to pray for them, "and for those others of whom we have spoken, for they be in sore need of prayer and help to uplift them—I speak of their sometime Chief in that dark City of the Mines, and also of the others of whom we have told you. Could earth people come to realise what they might do for those in the Hells, they would lessen, by their prayers for them, the ills they themselves suffer. For by lifting those poor spirits more into the light, and softening their anguish, they would lessen both the numbers and the malice of those who rush to earth to trouble those of like nature with themselves, and, through them, the whole of mankind.

"It is well for men to look upward and strive towards the light.

It is of more virtue to look downwards towards those who have sore need of strength so they may rise out of their unhappy spheres. For, bethink you, friend, this the Christ did long ago, and thus they do today."

I can give you only a fraction of the graphic story of the Hells, and a still smaller fraction of the remainder of Vale Owen's book, I think it quite a tragedy that it should be out of print; but, if you are interested, send a postcard to the Agents—Messrs. A. P. Watt & Son, Hastings House, Norfolk Street, W.C.2. Presumably, if they get enough postcards, they will arrange for a new edition to be printed.

Private Dowding's visit to Hell was something of a fiasco. He writes: "A soldier had been killed who was a degenerate, a murderer, a sensualist. He died cursing God and man. My brother had been told to rescue him. He took me with him. An angel of light came to protect us, otherwise we should have been lost in the blackness of the pit. The darkness grew. There was a strange allurement about the atmosphere. I thought we were lost.

At moments I hoped we were lost. So strong is the attraction.

Something sensual within me leaped and burned. I should have been lost without the angel's and my brother's help. We descended deeper. As a matter of fact I never reached the point where the rescue was attempted. I waited for their return in what seemed to be a deep, dark forest. The angel said that was the most insidious kind of hell, stagnation, because no one recognised it as such. That part of hell visited by my brother was brilliantly lighted. The light is coarse, artificial. It keeps out the light of God.

"All this my brother told me afterwards. Those who die filled with the thoughts of sensuality are attracted down the long, grey avenues.

The darkness appals. At last, light is seen ahead. It is the lure of hell. Some of these thoughts came to me whilst I waited in that gloomy forest. Then the angel and my brother returned. They had found him for whom they sought. He would not come away. Fear held him. He said his existence was awful, but he was afraid to move for fear worse conditions befell." I have abbreviated considerably, but I think that this account is illuminating in explaining why any soul should deliberately advance into the darkness of hell, when he might remain, at the worst, in Sphere One. Arnel would not feel the stirrings of lust as Private Dowding did, and so might not mention this very significant point.

The "Living Dead Man" mentions the Hells in a somewhat perfunctory way. He is not much interested in them or in the "Christian Heaven." He claims to have visited a Hell of fire and brimstone, and he says that there are individual hells of drunkenness and of lust and of hatred and of untruthfulness, and gives us a bloodcurdling account of a ghoul battening on the gin-soaked breath of a young man in a public house and goading him on to further excesses. But he is not very precise, and, even if we take him at his face value, he does not add much to our knowledge.

CHAPTER 10

LIFE IN HEAVEN

N ow I must try to give you some sort of outline of the rest of The Life Beyond the Veil. It is not easy to compress this into a small compass since the book runs to nearly 300,000 words, but I will do my best.

Vale Owen's mother fills most of the first volume with her personal experiences. She naturally does not profess to know more than she has been taught, but this part is interesting because it can be compared with the experiences of other spirits who are comparatively close to earth conditions.

The last part of Volume I is occupied by material supplied by a spirit called Astriel. Astriel was the headmaster of a school in Warwick in the time of George the First, and his short series of messages are among the most interesting in the book. He speaks on the interconnection of Science with Religion, and the picture which I gave of the Spheres was principally taken from him. He deals with Astronomy and Physics, and the mechanism of Prayer and Inspiration.

In Volume II the communicator throughout is a spirit named Zabdiel. He is perhaps the most remote of the communicating spirits and gives no account of his earth life. He defines the theme of his Course of Instruction as "That of the development of evil and good, and of God's present and future purpose with the Church of Christ and, throughout, of mankind generally." But, in fact, his messages cover a wide field, and contain a good deal of description of life and work in the higher spheres. In one passage he explains the meaning of some of our nursery tales. The story of Jack and the Beanstalk, for instance, originated in the Book of Revelations and St. John became Jack, who makes his ascent by means of Jacob's Ladder, which has become the Beanstalk. He writes: "The story I have named is one of many. Punch and Judy might represent the transactions in which the two who stood out most reprobate were Pilate and Iscariot. And from the manner in which these solemn, and indeed awful, incidents are related, the levity of the age in such matters is apparent.

"Well, so it is, and has been ever. But now, today, the spiritual is returning among men to claim a place, if not adequate to its importance, at least of greater consideration than of these last centuries." Zabdiel is always very grave and dignified, and at the end of his messages he is transferred beyond Sphere Ten, and so out of normal range of communication with earth. He takes leave of Vale Owen in a moving message, promising always to keep in touch with him.

I think that Zabdiel was, in fact, Vale Owen's Guardian Angel.

The third volume opens with messages from Kathleen and some friends of hers. It then settles down to a series of messages attributed to "Leader" for want of a better name. Spirits, ever since Jacob wrestled with the Angel, are habitually chary of giving their names—a proclivity which I shall later discuss—but this leads sometimes to confusion and misunderstanding. The "Leader" messages were eventually attributed to Arnel (who led the expedition through the Hells), but Zabdiel was occasionally referred to as "Leader," and this was confusing, though not perhaps of any very great importance.

Arnel, then, is the principal contributor to the last two volumes.

It is impossible to summarise the headings under which Arnel gives his messages, he covers almost every subject at one time or another.

He is perhaps a little less austere and remote than Zabdiel, and he is fond of slipping in a quaint little parable from time to time.

Towards the end of Volume 4 he gives a series of illuminating messages dealing with the future of this earth. He expects, but is not sure, that he may be placed in charge of the future development of the large company of souls which he was instrumental in rescuing from Hell.

I shall not give a fair picture of the book if I omit to give an impression of the extent to which descriptions of Manifestations and Displays have place therein. The descriptions are often prefaced by a deprecatory statement that human words cannot describe Celestial glories, and that colours exist beyond our octave of vision.

I think that this is very true, and, if I give you a sample of each you will get a very fair idea of the rest.

I give you first a description of a Manifestation seen by Vale Owen's mother and some recently arrived souls: — "By and by we were all assembled, and then we heard a burst of music which seemed to invade us all and unify the whole great multitude into one great family. Then we saw a great cross of light appear. It seemed to lie on the slope of the great mountain which bordered the plain and, as we watched it, it began to break up into specks of bright light, and we gradually became aware that it was a large company of angels of a higher sphere who stood on the mountain in the form of a cross; and all about them was a golden glow, which we could feel at that distance as a warm breath of love.

"Gradually they became more distinct to our vision as they emerged more perfectly into this, to them, lower environment, and then we saw, standing over the square where the arms of the cross joined the stem, a larger Being. We all seemed to know Him at once instinctively. It was a Manifestation of the Christ in what you have come to know as the Presence Form.

"He stood there silent and still for a long time, and then lifted His right hand on high, and we saw a column of light descend and rest upon it as He held it aloft. This column was a pathway, and on it we saw another company descending and, when they came to the uplifted hand, they paused and stood still with their hands folded on their breasts and heads bowed. Then slowly the hand moved out until it had swung round and down and the fingers pointed over the plain, and we saw the column stretch out towards us in mid-heaven until it bridged the space between the mountain and the plain, and the end of it rested over the multitude gathered there.

"Along this column walked the company last become visible, and hovered above us. They spread out their hands then, and all slowly turned towards the mountain, and softly we heard their voices half-speaking and half-singing a hymn of devotion to Him Who stood there all so beautiful and so holy that at first we were awed into silence. But presently we also took up their words and sang, or chanted, with them; for that evidently was their purpose in coming to us. And as we sang there arose between us and the mountain a mist of bluish tint which had a very curious effect. It seemed to act like a telescope lens, and brought the vision of Him nearer until we could see the expression on His face. It also acted similarly on the forms of those who stood just below Him. But we had no eyes for them, only for His gracious face and form. I cannot describe the expression. It was a blend of things which words can only tell in small part. There were blended love and pity and joy and majesty, and I felt that life was a very sacred thing when it held Him and us in one bond. I think others felt something like this too, but we did not speak to one another, all our attention being taken up with the sight of Him.

"Then slowly the mist melted into the atmosphere, and we saw the cross on the mountain and Him standing as before, only seen more dimly; and the angels who had come over to us had gone, and hovered above Him. And then all gradually faded away. But the effect was a very definite sense of His Presence remaining and perpetual." The blue mist which has the quality of enlarging the object looked at is mentioned in the description of the Hall of Evolution and in other places also.

On another occasion Zabdiel says: "I once observed a very beautiful instance of the transmutation of energy here in my own land.

"There was a company of visitors from another sphere, and they were about to return to their own, their mission having been finished. A party of our own, of whom I was one, went with them to the large lake over which they had come to us. Here they embarked in boats, and were giving us their parting words of thanks and goodwill, when one of our Princes was seen approaching with a company of attendants from behind us. They came through the air and hovered about us and the boats while we, knowing their habits, but not their present intention, waited to see what manner of thing they—or rather he had in his mind to do. For it is a delight in these realms to give pleasure, each to other, by exercising such powers as we possess, and that in varying combinations by which effects are differently produced.

"Far up in the heavens we saw them, as they moved slowly, circling about the Prince from whom to those in circle went threads and vibrations of different quality, and so of different colour. These he of his will sent forth, and those of his subordinates wove them into a network of curious design and very beautiful; and where two threads crossed, there the intensified light shone like a stone of brilliant hue. And the knots were of many colours owing to the varying combination of threads entering into their construction.

"When this was complete the circle widened out and drew away and left their Prince in the midst. And he held the net by its middle in his hand, and it floated out around him like a many coloured spider-web. It was very beautiful.

"Now, that net was really a system of many qualities of vibrations woven together. He loosed it of his hand and it began slowly to sink as he rose through it, until it was level with his feet. And as he came he looked through the net at the boats below; and he made slow movements with his hands in their direction.

"Then they began to move on the water as of themselves, and so continued until they floated in a circle. Then the net descended over them, and we saw that they were within its circumference, and also that, as it lighted upon them, they passed through it and it sank and rested upon the water. Then the Prince, standing on the net and on the water, in the midst of the boats, waved his hand in greeting to them. And the net slowly arose from the water, lifting the boats with it, and floated upwards into the air.

"So away over the lake they went together, and the company of our sphere closed in around them, and sent up a song of God-speed as they floated away towards the horizon over the lake." It seems not unlikely that Raymond was present at a Manifestation, although, as already stated, the experience was regarded as being too sacred for publication. Julia records a personal Manifestation at the beginning of her book, but Philemon says: "I have not yet seen—I have sensed with closed eyes a glory that I dared not yet gaze upon." That strange character the "Living Dead Man" writes: " I have met the Master from Galilee and have held converse with Him." I wonder? I have mentioned the difficulty of transmitting names in spirit messages, and the reluctance with which they are sometimes given, even when transmission is possible. The difficulty is obviously genuine, it is mentioned a dozen times in Vale Owen's book, "Cleophas" says: "... drawing from the words I do find in this floating mind that is about the handmaid. (Miss Cummins.) It containeth many words, so I shape my tale in the words I thus find. It is a mirror which is more than a glass; if there were not words within the handmaid's mind, the thought we cast upon the still pool would not be imagined there. So it is hard for us to give you a word or a name that doth not lie within her memory." As a matter of fact anyone who reads the Scripts of Cleophas will congratulate him upon the way in which he has overcome that particular obstacle.

As regards reluctance to give Celestial names, as opposed to difficulty in giving them, Zabdiel writes: "There is much power in the use of a name. Know this and remember it; for much disaster continually ensues by reason of the misuse of holy names, disaster wondered at and often felt to be unmerited." And Arnel: "Names are, therefore, had in reverence, not only in economies of earth, but in these heavenly realms also. For he who names a great angel Lord compromises that person with whatever work he has afoot to do. This is so ordained; and the highest of all, His Name, must be had in deepest reverence as in your own sacred law it is also enjoined." Spirits seem to be rechristened after a time, but not necessarily at once. It is strange to read of "A spirit named Elliotson" in *More Spirit Teachings* among the Theophiluses and Rectors and Philosophuses. I haven't seen the system of nomenclature discussed, or how they manage to avoid confusion with a single name.

As a matter of fact there seem to be two Imperators even in my limited bibliography—the author of *Spirit Teachings* (who was Malachi on earth, and associated with Nehemiah in the rebuilding of Jerusalem) and Caesar Augustus Imperator who helped the old monks with their Latin in The Gate of Remembrance, and called the communicators "Stultissimi barbari." The "Recording Angel" is not an individual but a mighty Registry. Every prayer, and every cry for help, even from the deepest hells, is registered, filtered and passed onward to its ultimate destination: and the same applies to ordinary and casual events in earth life. The problem of language is puzzling. From many indications, one would suppose that speech and language died out and communication was carried on by a species of thought-transference.

But this leaves unexplained passages such as the following: "Messages are received from those Spheres, transcribed into the language of Sphere Eleven, and dealt with there." Or: "He spoke to them in a language which I did not understand." Long passages are devoted to Astronomy and Physics. I lack space to quote, but I must make an exception for this passage; "On the other planets of your system are beings not unlike men.

On planets of other systems are beings not unlike men also. In other constellations there be those who are related reasonably to God and His Christ and can commune with their Creator, as do also men. But they are not of human form nor of human method of thought-communication which you call speech. And yet to them the Creator and His Christ stand in the same relation as they do to you." There is no such thing as blind force. The energy poured out by the sun is of spiritual generation and the same applies to all light and power throughout the universe. New worlds are continually being made and populated.

I would suggest that our own physicists might find in these books some clues to help them in their investigations into the ultimates of matter and energy, but unfortunately not all the science passages are on the same level. Zabdiel's course may not have taken him through the Halls of Science, and he gives vent to some remarkable statements on light and heat on page 130 of Volume II in which the properties of transmitters and reflectors appear to be confused. Of course he may be right, but, if so, many a schoolboy has been unjustly punished.

While we are dealing with physics, I might say that Sound apparently has the curious property of requiring less modification than light to be perceptible in the two worlds. One would have supposed that noise operates only through air, and so would be quite incommunicable to the other world; but apparently this is not so. Colonel Gascoigne writes: "It is very interesting for us to watch the result Hitler is producing through the noise of his bombs. . . . Every sound has its repercussions on the ether." And Private Dowding: "When a shell that took life exploded, then the sensation of it came much nearer to me. The noise and tumult came over the border-line with the lives of the slain." As regards the creation of structures and buildings, there is a complete account of the building of a Temple or Laboratory in Sphere Five. It is given by Arnel, but is much too long to quote.

The salient point is that: "it is not put together in bricks nor blocks as of stone on earth, but grows of a piece in one together." The design is first made, and then a company of builders under a powerful leader concentrate their minds creatively on the foundations, and gradually and very slowly raise the stream of their willpower from the ground up to the roof, and produce the outer building complete in outline but faint and of transient duration. This is repeated many times, the company spacing themselves equally around, until the outer shell is completed in form and solidified.

Then the interior construction is undertaken in a similar manner, and finally the interior decorations and ornaments are attended to.

The leader attends to the final inspection and correction of details, and finally a great Angel Lord comes down to perform the ceremony of Consecration.

This creation by will-power is universal in the higher spheres, and animals and flowers can be similarly formed; but it seems that in the lower spheres more mundane methods of building are employed. Raymond speaks of bricks being made out of emanations rising from the earth, and, in the Hells, stone and wood is apparently quarried and hewn as on earth.

The kind of clothing worn seems to vary with the spiritual status of the wearer. Lower or earth-bound spirits wear the sort of clothes to which they were accustomed on earth, or else some kind of "fancy-dress" if it amuses them. More highly developed spirits seem to wear robes rather in the classical style with gems which denote the order and degree of their Ministry. The colours vary with the personality of the wearer and his environment.

Angels adapt their forms and clothing on occasions for purposes of recognition or to meet the expectations of newly-arrived spirits, The angel who came to fetch Julia from her death-bed, for instance, appeared with wings; not because the wings were of any particular use, but because Julia expected angels to have wings and would not readily have recognised her visitor as such without them. But perhaps this is too definite. Philemon says that they are "appendages that supplement spiritual faculties that belong to some orders of angelic beings and not to others. And again; "I use my 'wings' to become a 'Christmas-card angel' to a dying youth who would be surprised at seeing only a man like his old Rector when he 'died.' And I leave aside my wings when a swearing, cursing, valiant atheist is thrust into the unseen. The wings would be regarded as 'darned flummery.' So I, assume a sober clerical garb and mien—I am giving you a fact of experience—and my atheist says: 'I always said parsons would find themselves in the hottest part of hell, and here if the first person I see is not a 'Holy Joe'! Old chap, I am sorry for you, and I'm real grieved to see a decent old gent like you here.' We became friends, and that man will race me, and perhaps outrun me, in the spiritual contest." Who says there is no humour in Heaven? The education of children is very carefully organised, especially that of the still-born and unborn. The sin of deliberate abortion and its punishment are strongly emphasised.

The future of the earth and its spiritual development are dealt with at length at the end of Vale Owen's book. Very briefly, the prophecy is that woman's influence, as typified by mother-love, will increase and, after some set-backs due to woman's attempts to lead and rule, earth life will accept woman's guidance (but not dominance) to the great benefit of all.

Religion, of course, is extensively discussed in most of the books which I have read, but I propose to keep this for my concluding chapter. All that I wish to say at this stage is that, whatever assaults are made upon our cherished dogmas, agreement is virtually unanimous that the only hope of the world lies in the imitation of Christ's life and the acceptance of His teaching.

Now I must tell you of some of the things which have perplexed me in the account of the afterlife given in Vale Owen's book. The first time

I read it I made a long list of things which appeared incomprehensible or incongruous: but on going through the book again and again, these difficulties mostly faded away or fell into place.

If I say that the following puzzlements remain, I do not mean that they are inexplicable, only that they are unexplained.

Firstly there is the existence of animals in Heaven. Bird life seems to be general, and horses, oxen and other animals not only exist but are put to use. Raymond, Philemon and Private Dowding speak of their dogs. If we suppose that birds are admitted for their ornamental value, and animals on account of their previous association with man, what happens to ugly carrion birds and the rest of the animal kingdom? How far down the scale do animals possess souls? Is the soul a prerogative of warm-blooded animals, or is it possessed by fish and insects? If by fish and insects, then by infusoria and germs? This may not be a matter of any great importance for man to understand, but it is a matter of great interest.

Next, there is mention of "people working in fields" in a comparatively high sphere, and of gardeners tending flowers. Who are these "people" whose labours are so terrestrial at such an advanced stage? What is the purpose of the fields, and what is grown in them? Then there is an apparently complete absence of any mechanical contrivance in Heaven: there is no mention of Railways or Motors or mechanical ships. This seems quite reasonable and natural.

Yet there are chariots and carts and ships propelled by sails and oars.

Another small puzzlement is the source of water circulation in the Spheres. There are rivers and lakes and seas and oceans, but no mention is made of clouds or rain in Life Beyond the Veil, though there is mention in another book of "places where it rains." A very great puzzle to the human mind is the general agreement of spiritual authorities on the subject of the existence of Elemental spirits; fairies, gnomes, pixies, elves, etc., in great variety and profusion. References to them are common in Vale Owen's book. In the last chapter Arnel gives a vision of the Grand Finale of the earth when the Christ Consummate appears. He writes: "Then out of this terrestrial light there came forth in their myriads all those half-rational forces which have their place among the elements of earth. These are very strange in their shapes and also in their movements. I had not seen these until now, and I was very greatly intent upon their manners. These I speak of were those impersonal forces which insure cohesion in minerals, and those by which the vegetation is enthused with its life, and those who were guardians of animals in their kinds. The mineral entities were not much sentient in themselves until magnetised by those great Lords of Creation whose province it was to sustain this realm in its orders.

But the vegetable entities had in themselves a formed and subjective faculty of sensation with which to respond to the forces poured upon them by their Rulers. . . . The animal entities, however, had fully sensation in themselves, and also a modicum of personality.

And their Lords were very splendid in their array." These Elementals exist, not only on earth, but in Heaven, up to the highest spheres described in any detail. Zabdiel speaks of Spirits of the Woodlands in Sphere Ten.

Private Dowding writes: "I have made friends with many of the water-fairies in the spring up on the mountain-side." The "Living Dead Man" speaks of a Parisian magician who kept a Sylph as a familiar spirit to help him in his work. When I read the *Living Dead Man* I am sympathetically reminded of Matilda's aunt in *Cautionary Tales*; perhaps you remember the lines: Her Aunt, who from her earliest youth Had held a strict regard for Truth, Attempted to believe Matilda.

The effort very nearly killed her.

However, I shall come to him very soon now, and I will postpone, till then, consideration of that most perplexing problem of all —Reincarnation.

A point which is difficult to understand, but which is obviously of the highest importance to mankind, is that it is stated to be actually harder to change one's opinions after than before death.

One would have supposed that it would be easy to cast aside bodily desires when there is no longer a compelling need to satisfy them, to forgive an enemy when he can no longer harm you, and to discard erroneous convictions in the light of fuller knowledge and instruction. Yet it seems that this is not the case. Zabdiel says: "For a longer or shorter period sometimes, and often indeed for some thousands of years, as you reckon time on earth, a man may maintain his obduracy." And, of an opinionated scientist: "Here he made a strenuous effort, and the good at length prevailed in him.

But it was a fierce and protracted fight, and one of much galling and bitter humiliation." I have already quoted the case of the poor Norwegian shopkeeper who found it so difficult to discard his hatred of the Germans.

So do not imagine that these matters can be neglected on earth and that everything can be set right without effort in the new light which will come beyond the grave. Keep a flexible mind and avoid cast-iron opinions.

I cannot say that I feel particularly well satisfied with this attempt to summarise Vale Owen's book and to correlate it with other messages, but if I had done more my own book would have become unwieldy. I do, however, earnestly advise fuller study by those who are able to obtain the works which I have cited.

CHAPTER 11

THE LIVING
DEAD MAN

A nd now for that puzzling character the "living dead man." I want to start by saying that his letters have no inherent right to acceptance or rejection more than any of the other messages which we have been considering.

I am excluding from all, equally, any suspicion of deliberate fraud or deception on the part of those who have given them to the world. In the first place this would be a most invidious task and might let me in for a libel action, and in the second place I think that the explanation is so unlikely as to be unworthy of serious consideration.

In this particular case, the explanation is more than ever unlikely. The amanuensis was an authoress, and as she points out in the Introduction, she had her own literary reputation to consider and did not wish for celebrity as a "freak." Here follow such extracts from the Introduction as will enable you to grasp the circumstances in which the messages were written.

"One night last year in Paris" (the book was published in 1914), "I was strongly impelled to take up a pencil and write, though what I was to write about I had no idea. Yielding to the impulse, my hand was seized as if from the outside, and a remarkable message of a personal nature came, followed by the signature 'X.'" The purport of the message was clear, but the signature puzzled me.

"The following day I showed this writing to a friend asking her if she knew who 'X' was.

" 'Why,' she replied, 'don't you know that that is what we always call Mr.-?' I did not know.

"Now Mr. -was six thousand miles from Paris, and as we supposed in the land of the living. But a day or two later a letter came to me from America, stating that Mr. -had died in the western part of the United States a few days before I received in Paris the automatic message signed 'X'." . . .

"To the whole subject of communication between the two worlds I felt an unusual degree of indifference. Spiritualism had always left me quite cold, and I had not even read the standard works on the subject." . . .

"Several letters signed 'X' were automatically written during the next few weeks; but instead of becoming enthusiastic, I developed a strong disinclination for this manner of writing, and was only persuaded to continue it through the arguments of my friend that if 'X' really wished to communicate with the world, I was highly privileged in being able to help him." . . .

"The messages continued to come. After a while there was no more lameness of the hand and arm, and the form of the writing became less irregular, though it was never very legible." ...

"While writing these letters I was generally in a state of semiconsciousness, so that, until I read the message over afterwards I had only a vague idea of what it contained." . . .

"When it was first suggested that these letters should be published with an introduction by me, I did not take very enthusiastically to the idea. Being the author of several books, more or less well known, I had my little vanity as to the stability of my literary reputation. I did not wish to be known as an eccentric, a 'freak'." . .

"That anyone would accuse me of deliberate deceit and romancing in so serious a matter did not then and does not now seem likely, my fancy having other and legitimate outlets in poetry and fiction."

" 'X' was not an ordinary person. He was a well-known lawyer nearly seventy years of age, a professional student of philosophy, a writer of books, a man whose pure ideals and enthusiasms were an inspiration to everyone who knew him." . . .

This being so, it seems essential that his messages should receive fair and dispassionate comment, in spite of their fundamental difference in outlook from that of the others which we have been considering. If "X" had been a man of unkindly and cynical character, it would be easy to dismiss the whole series as a sardonic practical joke, but this would not be justifiable. We must take the messages seriously and see if we can find any means of reconciling them with the others.

In the first place we must take account of the monumental selfconfidence of the man. Before his body is comfortably interred in California, his spirit is in Paris violently controlling the hand of his scribe to tell the world the secrets or the hereafter—but I had better give you a summary of the book first and draw conclusions afterwards.

In his second message "X" announces his intention of "coming back with power." This note runs throughout the book; he is going to learn all he can, and fix it indelibly in his mind, so that he will remember it after re-birth. Then he is going to choose his mother with great care, come back to earth as a Master and exercise spiritual powers which are normally hidden from humanity.

He has a Teacher—of course better than anyone else's. Most teachers are like University Professors, not much good, but his is a Master.

His scribe is not to allow any other spirits to communicate through her. He calls them "larvae of the astral world." His philosophy of Reincarnation is thus outlined: "A sudden memory of earth assails the spirit. How can the world get on without him? He is being left out of things. Oh for the iron grip of matter once more. Something to hold in taut hands. How can he return? Ah! he remembers. . . . He closes his eyes, reversing himself in the invisible. He is drawn to human life, to human beings in the intimate vibration of union. . . . He lets go his hold upon freedom and triumphantly loses himself in the lives of human beings.

"After a time he awakes to look upon the round solid faces of men and women. Sometimes he weeps, and wishes himself back.

If he becomes discouraged he may return—only to begin the weary quest of matter all over again.

"If he is strong and stubborn he remains and grows into a man. . . . After years enough he grows weary of the material struggle.

He sinks back into the arms of the unseen, and men say that he is dead. But he is not dead, he has only returned whence he came." On the subject of Service, he writes: "You will be interested to know that there are people out here, as on earth, who devote themselves to the welfare of others." He says that they work on a "rather more intellectual plane than the Salvation Army." He says that they have done good service, but obviously does not associate himself with them in any way.

He makes great friends with a boy called Lionel, "who calls me Father and seems to enjoy my society." Lionel is much interested in engineering and machinery. "He wants to go back and fly in an aeroplane. I tell him that he can fly here without one, but that does not seem to be the same thing to him. He wants to get his fingers on machinery. . . . The curious thing about it is that he can remember other and former lives of his on earth. . . . The boy was an inventor in a prior incarnation."

"X" takes Lionel for a "walk" in Paris, but the boy cannot see anything; "when I pointed out certain buildings to him, he asked me quite sincerely if I were dreaming. ... So when the boy found that Paris was only a figment of my imagination—I took him to see Heaven. He remarked: 'Why this must be the place my grandmother used to tell me about. But where is God?' "That I could not tell him; but, on looking again, we saw that nearly everybody was gazing in one direction. We also gazed with the others, and saw a great light, like a sun, only it was softer and less dazzling than the material sun.

" 'That,' I said to the boy, 'is what they see who see God.' "And now I have something strange to tell you; for as we gazed at that light, slowly there took form between us and it the figure which we are accustomed to see represented as that of the Christ. He smiled at the people and stretched out His hands to them.

"Then the scene changed, and He had on His left arm a lamb; and then again He stood as if transfigured upon a mountain; then He spoke and taught them. We could hear His voice. And then He vanished from our sight." You should note that "X" regards this, and similar experiences, as being something that goes on in the "Christians' Heaven," and as having no personal application to himself. "The Messiahs" are only for the weak. He is a strong soul who is going on, under his own steam, to become a Master (and perhaps a god).

While we are on the subject of Lionel, I had better finish with him. Lionel is now much interested in choosing a family of engineers in which to be born again. . . . "It is strange about this boy. Out in this world there is boundless opportunity to work in subtle matter, opportunity to invent and experiment; yet he wants to get his hands on iron and steel. Strange!" One day Lionel is resting in a little hut on a hillside and "X" from outside sees the hut all lit up with radiance from Lionel's personality. "It looked like a pearl lighted from within." So "X" goes inside and tells Lionel to go a little distance away and say if he sees anything. Lionel comes back and says: "What a wonderful man you are Father! How did you make that hut seem to be on fire?" This tribute is apparently accepted by "X" in smug silence.

Finally Lionel hears that his school teacher is going to marry an engineer—the elder brother of one of Lionel's school friends.

This is too good an opportunity to miss and Lionel dives back into earth life to the great regret of "X. "There is a chapter entitled "A Folio of Paracelsus."

"X" has asked his Teacher to give him a book dealing with exploration in the spirit world. The Teacher smiles and hands him a book.

"Who wrote this book?" I asked.

"There is a signature," he replied.

"I looked at the end and saw the signature. It was that used by Paracelsus." Now I don't know if there is any special significance in this little story, but why did the Teacher smile and answer evasively? Paracelsus was an imaginary name conferred upon himself by Theophrastus Bombastus von Hohenheim who lived in Switzerland and Germany in the sixteenth century. He was an alchemist and a physician, and wandered over a great part of Europe in pursuit of knowledge.

His characteristics are given as vanity, arrogance, aggressiveness and intense scientific and philosophical curiosity. A quaint notion has struck me; I wonder if the same idea has occurred to you. If not, no matter.

He speaks of the great variety of dress worn by the inhabitants of that "country." Clothes are made by will-power after the visualisation of a pattern. "X" wants to wear a Roman toga, and his Teacher helps him to make one. He meets a lady dressed in a Greek costume and cross-examines her rather intimately about her clothing. She answers politely but quite vaguely and is clearly not much interested.

There is a chapter about the horrible fascination exercised on some spirits by their own defunct bodies; and how they go back time after time to watch the process of disintegration. "X" says that he himself has been "back a few times," but warns others against indulgence in this propensity.

He says that the happiest spirits of his acquaintance are the artists— painters, poets and musicians. He says: "Of all earthly things, sound reaches most directly into this plane of life." This bears out what has been already said elsewhere.

"X" writes: "I am often called upon here to decide matters for others. Many people call me 'The Judge'." A widower who has married again is claimed by both his earthly wives simultaneously, while he is looking for his sweetheart whom he prefers to either of them. "X" solves their problem by quoting Christ's answer to the Sadducees about there being no marrying nor giving in marriage. This dictum apparently comes as a complete surprise to the disputants; and, while it does not completely solve their problem, it provides them with a basis for a compromise.

"X" is sorry for the man; he says: "Perhaps the only way in which he can get free from his too insistent companions is to go back to earth." He knows of a way, however, by which solitude might be secured: he could build round himself a wall "which only the eyes of a great initiate can pierce." He adds: "I have not told this secret to my friend, but perhaps I shall someday, if it seems necessary for his development that he should have a little solitude." Here follows a fairly complete summary of "X's" intentions: "I purpose, for instance, in a few years not only to pick up a general knowledge of the conditions of this four-dimensional world, but to go back over my other lives and assimilate what I learned in them. I want to make a synthesis of the complete experiences of my ego up to this date, and to judge from that synthesis what I can do in the future with least resistance. I believe, but I am not quite sure, that I can bring back much of this knowledge with me when I am born again.

"I shall try to tell you—or some of you—when and about where to look for me again. Oh, don't be startled. It will not be for some time yet. An early date would necessitate hurry, and I do not wish to hurry. I could probably force the coming back, but that would be unwise, for I should then come back with less power than I want. ... I shall not do, however, as many souls do; they stay out here until they are as tired of this world as they formerly were tired of the earth, and then they are driven back half unconsciously by the irresistible force of the tide of rhythm. I want to guide that rhythm." And later: "Of course I cannot swear now to remember everything when I come into heavy matter again; but I am determined to do so if possible; and I shall succeed to some extent if I do not get the wrong mother. I intend to take great care on that point, and to choose a mother who is familiar with the idea of rebirth.

If possible I want to choose a mother who actually knew me in my last life as-, and who, if I shall announce in childhood that I am that same-whom she knew as a young girl, will not chide me and drive me back into myself with her doubts."

About "rhythm" he says: "Do get this idea of rhythm into your brain. All beings are subject to the law of rhythm, even the gods —though in a greater way than ourselves with longer periods of flex and reflex." He says: "Eternity is a circle, a serpent that swallows its own tail." He again manifests intense anxiety that his scribe shall operate for none but himself. He says: "Furthermore, I advise you never, even at the urgent prayer of those whose loved ones have gone out —never to lend yourself to them." All messages are unanimous on the terrible consequences of suicide. "X" writes: "I can only say with regard to suicide, that if men knew what awaits those who go out by their own hand they would remain with the evil that they know."

"X" is surprised to find that there are no shadows in his world.

It is explained to him that: "We light our own place. How could our forms cast shadows, when light radiates from them in all directions?" Elsewhere "X" explains that daytime on earth is his night; he can see in the dark, but not in sunlight which is too "coarse in its vibrations" for his eyes.

In his twenty-sixth letter, "X" speaks of energy thus: "Why it takes more energy on earth to put one heavy foot before another, and to propel the hundred or two-hundred-pound body a mile, than it takes here to go around the world!" And later: "By and by, before I return to the world, I shall review these reviews, fixing by will the memories which I specially wish to carry over with me. . . . Also I want to take with me the knowledge of certain formulae, and the habit of certain practices which you would probably call occult; by means of which I can call into memory this very pageant of experience which now rolls before me whenever I will it."

"X" still "stays himself occasionally with a little nourishment," an infinitesimal amount compared with the beef steak dinners which he used to eat.

"X" deprecates "spirit-hunting" by foolish or irresponsible people. He says: "I wish to go on record as discouraging irresponsible mediumship." His reason is that vagrant and undesirable spirits, or even elementals, may take the opportunity of communicating.

The story of the Sylph and the Magician, which I mentioned in the last chapter, comes in the thirtieth letter. At the end of this story, "X" has a passing qualm about his own philosophy of indefinite rebirth. He says: "I rather dread to go back into the world, where it will be so dull for me for a long time. Can exchange this freedom and vivid life for a long period of somnolence, afterwards to return to such a battle and learn the multiplication table and Greek and Latin verbs? I suppose I must—but not yet." In the next letter "X" asks his Teacher about Sylphs and other elementals, and if they ever become human. The Teacher does not know; he thinks they are all working in the direction of man, but that they will not reach this stage in the present life cycle.

Perhaps the most puzzling character in this most puzzling book is that of the "Beautiful Being," who adopted "X" as a companion on various journeys to earth and promised to be his guide on a later inter-planetary journey. The Being is an angel, sometimes seeming to be male and sometimes female. "X" says: "Imagine youth immortalised, the fleeting made eternal. Imagine the bloom of a child's face, and the eyes of the ages of knowledge. Imagine the brilliancy of a thousand lives concentrated in those eyes, and the smile upon the lips of a love so pure that it asks no answering love from those it smiles upon." "X," usually so introspective and self-contained, becomes quite lyrical about the Being. He calls him "the fairy who makes blind babies dream of daisy-fields"; and again he says: "I wish I could explain the influence of the Beautiful Being. It is unlike anything else in the universe. It is elusive as a moon beam, yet more sympathetic than a mother. It is daintier than a rose, yet it looks upon ugly things with a smile. It is purer than the breath of the sea, yet it seems to have no horror or impurity. It is artless as a child, yet wiser than the ancient gods, a marvel of paradoxes, a celestial vagabond, the darling of the unseen." His enthusiasm is positively embarrassing.

In a company they watch a "midnight revel in a haunt of vice," without being "shocked or horrified." I suppose that the nearest analogy to the Beautiful Being that one could think of would be the spirit of the god Pan.

"X's" Teacher moralises on his work as follows: "Do not think that I am indifferent to the sufferings of the weakest ones because I give my time and attention to the strong. Like the ministering angels, I go where I am most needed. Only the strong ones can learn what I have to teach. The weak ones are the charges of the Messiahs and their followers. But nevertheless, between us and the Messiahs there is brotherhood and there is mutual understanding. Each works in his own field. The Messiahs help the many; we help the few. Their reward in love is greater than ours; but we do not work for reward any more than they do. Each follows the law of his being."

"X" describes how he has seen spirits lying in a state of unconsciousness more profound than the deepest sleep. He asks who these are, and his Teacher replies: "They are those who in their earth life denied the immortality of the soul. They will awaken centuries, perhaps ages, hence, when the irresistible laws of rhythm shall draw them out of their sleep into incarnation." One of them is selected for premature resuscitation for the edification of "X," on the assurance that his curiosity is purely scientific and not activated by pity. The man is told that he has been asleep for ninety-five years, and asks how long he would have slept had he not been awakened. He is told: "Probably until those who had started even with you had left you far behind on the road of evolving life." He must submit himself to training and then go back to earth to convert to the truth of immortality as many men as he had previously deluded by his false doctrines.

The reasoning in this letter is not very convincing. If unconsciousness is complete, five minutes and five thousand years are equal fractions of infinity, and neither is any particular punishment; if indeed the soul should be punished at all for choosing one erroneous belief out of the many available in this life, and, apparently in the next also.

The next letter is devoted to explaining that there are many gods in the world's pantheons, and that "the realities exist out ere." You will note that god is spelt with a small g, and I think that what "X" calls gods are in fact the same as the great Angel Lords described in Vale Owen's book as being in charge of the heavenly Departments. The only idea that a Christian would consider blasphemous is that a man can become a god by developing god-consciousness. "X's" personal ideas on the subject may be gauged from the following passage: "Who do you fancy will be the gods of the future cycles of existence? Will they not be those who, in this cycle of planetary life, have raised themselves above the mortal? Will they not be the strongest and most sublime among the present spirits of men? Even the gods must have their resting period, and those in office now would doubtless wish to be supplanted." I told you earlier about the woman who lived in a boarding house and complained of the coffee, but I did not tell you how "X" disposed of her. He did so by the simple process of taking her to the "orthodox Christian heaven"; having prepared her for the experience with the advice: "The great thing in Heaven is to love all the others. That is what makes them happy." With little more spiritual equipment than this he leaves her; for, as he somewhat naively remarks: "I wanted to leave her in such way that she would not come out again to look for me." Next there is a letter warning us about evil spirits and the vicarious pleasure which they obtain by attaching themselves to us during our moments of hate, anger or avarice. Here is a quotation: s "Sometimes the impersonal interest in mere strife becomes personal; an angry spirit here may find that by attaching himself to a certain man he is sure to get every day a thrill or thrills of angry excitement, as his victim continually loses his temper and storms and rages. This is one of the most terrible misfortunes which can happen to anybody. Carried to its ultimate, it may become obsession, and end in insanity." I mentioned the man who said he was Shakespeare, and the playacting habits of earth-bound spirits. These are very tolerantly regarded, "There are no penalties inflicted by the community for the personating of one man by another. It is not taken seriously, for to the clear sight of this world the disguise is too transparent." Towards the end of his message "X" seems to lose a little of his superior attitude towards the Christian idea. He writes: "Last night I went to one of the highest Christian heavens. Perhaps I could not have gone so easily at any other time; for my heart was full of love for all men and my mind was full of the Christ idea.

Often have I seen Him who is called the Saviour of men, and last night I saw Him in all His beauty. . . . Jesus is a type of the greatest Master. He is revered in all the heavens. He grasped the Law, and dared to live it, to exemplify it." Later "X" describes how he put himself into a sort of trance for a week, after having ensured through his Teacher that he would wake up punctually.

He says: "There is nothing but loveliness in that sleep ... I found there the simulacrum of everyone I had ever loved ... I refound too my old dreams of ambition and enjoyed the fruit of all my labour on earth. . . . Rest! on earth you know not the meaning of the word. I rested only seven days; but so refreshed was I that had I not other worlds to conquer, I should almost have had the courage to return to earth." The next letter is a sermon, preached mainly on the text of letting go all earthly ties as soon as possible after death. "Get away from the world just as soon as you can." (Incidentally this seems rather inconsistent with "X's" own philosophy of preparing continuously for a "return with power.") There is no need to worry about influencing earth-dwellers for good. "The heavens above your head now are literally swarming with souls who long to take a hand in the business of earth, souls who cannot let go, who find the habit of managing other people's affairs a fascinating habit, as enthralling as that of tobacco or opium." In the same letter he says: "Do not invoke the spirits of the dead. They may be busy elsewhere." The next letter begins: "I met a charming woman the other night." This charming woman had always wanted a great deal of money; and when someone died and left her a fortune, she died of joy. Bad luck! Wasn't it? However, she appears to enjoy herself very much by touring in Egypt with her still-living husband, conversing with him by means of automatic writing.

"X" takes his leave on the eve of his inter-planetary tour with the Beautiful Being: "Think of it! I shall see far-away planets and meet their inhabitants. Shall I find the 'square-faced men'? Perhaps so." So ends this astonishing book, full of trivialities and inconsistencies, but with something about it which prevents its being swept aside as unworthy of analysis and consideration. For one thing it brings us up against the problem of Reincarnation as a subject which we cannot evade, even if we want to.

Here I get into deep waters and I cannot presume to express strong opinions on a subject on which so little has been revealed. I can only tabulate what is said in the works which I have studied.

Vale Owen's book scarcely mentions the subject, but it infers that animal spirits may eventually become human: "We saw the spirits of men who were in the animal stage." In answer to a question: "Would a memory of our past lives help us in our present one?" Colonel Gascoigne replies: "No, it would only produce confusion of thought and not render any real help to the life you were living. To some great souls who have progressed very far the memory of other lives is vouchsafed. Genius is often a memory from other lives. You see this force coming out in children whom you call prodigies, but, again, it is a returning memory." So, you see, Colonel Gascoigne takes Reincarnation for granted, and has later specifically confirmed his opinion.

Both Julia and Philemon speak of a partial Reincarnation They both use the same metaphor—the hub and spokes of a wheel Julia says: "There is not any total plunge into matter again; or ever. The hub of the wheel is here, but the spoke is incarnate.

. . . We are fashioned spoke by spoke till we can all be fitted into the perfect round. ... A spoke may be reincarnated again and again. Sometimes it is never again passed through the gateway of birth. . . . Yes, it is possible for the Hub to be in Heaven and the Spoke in Hell. . . . Sometimes there is more than one Spoke incarnate at the same time. ... As for you, your Spoke, now incarnated, has been incarnate before, many times. And there are other Spokes." All very puzzling, isn't it? Philemon writes: "I am beginning to think that there may be truth in a wild idea, as I then thought, which W. T. Stead told me: that the ego—the spirit—was the hub of a wheel and that our varying personalities are the earth-bound form of the central self." This is quite possibly a legacy from an earth-conversation (because you will remember that it was Stead who was Julia's amanuensis).

He continues: "I wish to leave no lesson of earth life unlearned, so that I need not fear rebirth in the flesh. I have never denied even its probability, still less its possibility. I rebelled against it. It is a deep-rooted antagonism in my very being, and that you must take into consideration when I express my views on this matter." A plausible theory (but apparently only a theory) is outlined thus: "Souls which will not, cannot, conceive of other earth-life may gravitate to the earth-spheres and become again human infants in the arms of human parents. But it is not a necessity. I know that it is not a necessity so far as I have gone in the new life.

Hopelessly perverse souls may be given the chance of rebirth on earth, but it is tantamount to starting all over again." He finishes up with the final dictum: "Reincarnation as taught is not true, yet pre-existence is a truth." Which doesn't help us very much.

Here is something more definite. It is from a book called *The Life Elysian*, by R. J. Lees. The message comes from a comparatively immature spirit, but one who claims to have been specially selected and trained as an instructor to humanity. It reads: "Among the souls who are still subjected to earth conditions— from whom all experiences have to be received with caution, and not acted upon until they are confirmed from more reliable sources—there are many who honestly think reincarnation to be a fact, and teach it to be so.

"Among those who have passed away from these conditions and learned to accept truth for its own sake ... I have been unable to meet with one holding the theory of rebirth to be true. The origin of the idea is to be found in savage superstition." And later: "No! The theory of reincarnation is one of the devices invented by priests to terrify men and women into subjection; it could not possibly be introduced into the natural order of existence without reducing the whole system to chaos." It is strange that such a long and didactic book as *Spirit Teachings* should give us so little help on this subject; Imperator does say however: "The Egyptians' doctrine of transmigration through vast ages and cycles was an error which symbolised and typified eternal and unceasing progress." Finally there is a book called *Beyond Human Personality*, communicated through Miss Geraldine Cummins by that same Frederic Myers whom I have previously mentioned in connection with the book *Raymond*. Myers teaches that the Third Sphere (or Summerland as it is often called in spiritualist circles) is in fact a sphere of Illusion inhabited for long or short periods by souls whose mentalities are still dominated by Earth-conditions, more sublimated, and with the difference that the struggle for existence is no longer operative and souls can gratify every harmless desire merely by the expression of a wish. "On earth he longed for a superior brand of cigar. He can have the experience and the scenery and the flora and fauna are all similar to those of earth, and here the soul lives a life similar to that of earth, but nauseam of smoking this brand. He wanted to play golf, so he plays golf. But he is merely dreaming all the time, or rather living within the fantasy created by his strongest desires on earth." In this effortless and purposeless existence, no real progress is made, and the soul whose desires are preponderatingly animal, soon yearns for further existence in heavy matter and is reincarnated on earth or sometimes in another similar planetary life. (This supports what was said by the Living Dead Man.) But the soul who is more spiritually inclined passes upward into the Fourth Sphere and thenceforward progresses continuously without any further individual reincarnation.

This book is well worth reading because Myers in earth-life had devoted much of his time to a philosophic study of human personality and its survival of bodily death, and produced a standard work on the subject. It is however rather too abstruse for extensive quotation in a simple book like this.

It is really astonishing! One would say that Reincarnation is either a fact or not a fact, and that there could not be two opinions about it on the other side. If it is a fact, there must be a continuous avalanche of spirits sliding back into earth-life and leaving gaps which must be noticeable by everyone; and if it is not a fact, how has the delusion spread so widely among the spirits closest to earth-life and so, presumably, in the best position to watch what is going on? One thing, however, seems to be quite certain (if one can say that anything is certain because it is consonant with human reasoning and intelligence) and that is that the crude system of reincarnation described by "X" must be untrue. The obvious flaw is that spirits should be able to choose their new mothers without an independent control.

Can you imagine the crowd of emulous snob-spirits struggling for priority at a ducal wedding, or the boycotting of some humble proletarian union? I suppose that I must not shirk giving my own opinion about the Living Dead Man book as a whole. I offer my ideas with all diffidence.

In the first place, it seems to me to be diametrically opposed to the spirit of all the other books which we have considered that "X" should be able to make any important advance in the spirit world, actuated as he is by motives or self-seeking and ambition.

It is true that he occasionally helps other spirits, but in a patronising and superior way, and more to get rid of them than from any motive of real kindness. His interests lie in and near the earth, and it seems distinctly possible that he will in fact be reincarnated (perhaps in company with countless other earth-bound spirits) though possibly not in such agreeable circumstances as he plans for himself.

Against this we must set his high character in earth-life, and the exceptional consideration which appears to be accorded to him by his Teachers and others.

The following quotation from Philemon may possibly be apposite: "I know that ambitious beings, once men, desirous of domination, are playing upon minds of similar type. The deification of the intellect to the neglect of the heart is the main defect of modern Theosophy." Those of us who look forward to an orderly progress via the "Christian Heavens" need not be unduly disturbed by this book, because "X" does not question their existence nor their regular operation; and if on that account we have to classify ourselves in "X's" estimation among the "weak ones" who are the care of the "Messiahs," I hope that we shall have enough humility not to let that disturb us unduly.

What really is so disturbing about the book is the idea that we may, by forming strong opinions on inadequate data here on earth, actually divert the course of our future life into a particular channel which we should not have followed if we had been aware of the facts.

While/therefore, I am convinced that it is consonant with duty and wisdom to seek and examine all available evidence about the future life, I am sure that we ought not to form dogmatic opinions, but to maintain a degree of humility and flexibility of thought so that we may readily accept and absorb the Truth when it is eventually made known to us.

CHAPTER 12

LOOSE ENDS

I want here to tidy up a few loose ends before I go on to my final chapter dealing with the impact of spirit communications on Religion.

In the first place I want to tell you about a little book which I have not hitherto mentioned. It is called *Letters from Lancelot* and a limited number of copies are still available from Mrs. Tristram, Cox's Mill, Dallington, Heathfield, Sussex, at the price of 3s. 4d. post free.

The reason why I have not mentioned it before is that the messages came from a little boy of eight, and they are written to his "Mum" in baby language and with baby spelling. They are most terribly open to mockery and ridicule on that account, and I think that it is very brave and unselfish of the mother to give to the world such precious and intimate messages from her darling little boy.

"But, Mum, I didn't rite them for people to read in a book, I only wrote for my own, own Mum."

But if you arc prepared to read with love and understanding in your heart, get this book, and I can promise you a most wonderful treat. Things are revealed through this child which amplify in an astonishing way the somewhat pedestrian treatment which I have accorded to the other messages. Naturally, no knowledge of Hell conditions is allowed to reach this budding mind, and even one short visit to the sphere of the earth-bound fills Lancelot with desolation, but in other respects the revelations made through these baby messages surpass anything which I have recorded elsewhere.

Truly, "Out of the mouth of babes and sucklings thou has perfected praise." The merely curious will find descriptions of visits to other planets and other constellations, but it is not to the merely curious that the book is commended.

Lancelot wanders over this world, as well as others, on his voyages of exploration, and it is interesting to note that he is more astonished and impressed by seeing flying-fish (of which he had never heard) than by new forms of life on some unimaginably remote planet.

He throws fresh light on ectoplasm and elementals and other phenomena which have puzzled us for generations, but the most wonderful thing is the clear light which his baby language throws on the great spiritual truths. Death, to us, should not be a thing to be dreaded, but a "consummation devoutly to be wished" as soon as life's work is done.

One evening his mother spent in table tilting to convince a sceptical friend of the existence of unseen things. Lancelot writes: "I was rather cross wen you went all the evening being so silly with that table business wich is not a mind thing at all but only SILLY NONSENSE of force of ectoplasm wich can be used for moving anything if you don't want to push it properly, but it is SO SILLY to do that and not mean anything at all, and ectoplasm is very useful wen you know wot you want it for but just to make a table go bumping isn't a sensible thing to do at all, and Mum you might have been torking to ME instead." The odd thing is that though the messages go on for nearly three years, Lancelot's spelling does not improve very much. I suppose it is because he has no occasion to read English books. In one message he writes: "Mum, dont I spell right? I saw in your mind a thort about spelling. Yes, do tell me, and I can rite—write— slower, and watch your mind for the word after I've said it. . . .

Slow writing is best, then I can see my words come in your mind and you can spell for me. O mum, I am just a little boy still and you are so my mother." About ghosts, he writes: "Mum, I did want to say a thing for you to know about, and that is to say I have learnt wot those things we call ghosts are now, and it's ever so interesting becos it's like this— people give out a sort of fluid stuff called ectoplasm and they make a shape of it wich is like wot they looked like on earth in their earth form, and they don't want it after they first learn to do without it, so they often leave it off almost at once and then it goes on in the place ware they left it going on doing over again wot they last did with it, and it isn't anything to matter becos it's only ectoplasm wich is a sort of matter thing and not anything of mind at all. . . . Only the people who want not to die very much leave ectoplasms, the others just let it die in their bodies and go off straight away as spirits which is the sensible thing to do because ectoplasms are only a nuisance to everyone." And on the colour question: "Mum, you are so clear that I would like to say one more thing which is about people with colour —black and brown people I mean. They are awfully backward in most things but they get on simply splendidly here because they aren't so dependent on their brains but have more imagination and feelings, and they have to learn not to be AFRAID any more and then they go ahead like anything and beat the white ones HOLLOW sometimes." I think I will use one passage from Lancelot to deal with a subject which I postponed from Chapter 7; I mean the help given by spirits in the way of inspiration to men in their progress in the arts and sciences. My friend, if you remember, said: "No discovery in physics, chemistry or mathematics, no new idea in art or literature can be traced to our spirit guides." Now whenever this subject is mentioned by communicators, they are unanimous in stating that such help is not given by means of direct revelation. A discovery in wave-mechanics does not come to a political economist, still less to a dilettante frequenter of stances, but to a man who has been using his human brain on the subject up to the limits of its capacity.

Further, it is claimed that all the best music and poetry comes by way of inspiration to those who have worked to earn it, and the same is largely true about art.

To quote Lancelot: "I wish Dad was here becos I want to say a thing he would like, and that is that we often give men a help with their inventions of machinery and things of all sorts, becos its very good for men to use their human brains a lot, and so they get new ideas of how to make machinery and so on from us and they work it out, it gives things for their brains to use you see. I can't yet of course, but grandpapa does often help people like that." One other little quotation I must give. You remember that in Chapter 10 I mentioned, among those things which had perplexed me, the question: "How far down the scale do animals possess souls?" Here is Lancelot to the rescue: "I needn't go for a minit Mum, so I'll just say one more thing about fishes, that I can't see anything in them at all of mind and I don't know but I don't think they go on at all. I've looked and looked wen I see them, but there isn't anything of mind there or anything like animals on land sumtimes have or birds about their nests. Fishes Dont Have ANYthing at all of love or mind A Bit. I wonder why they don't?"

A valued friend who read the early part of this book in manuscript accused me of a Wellsian attitude in ignoring arguments on the other side. I can lay my hand on my heart and affirm that I have *tried* to be intellectually honest with you, but if there is justice in the accusation, I think that it arises from a misapprehension of my primary object, which is not to convince determined materialists as to the discarnate and spiritual sources of the messages, but to take existing messages and analyse and correlate them so as to see what sense we can make of them. After all, nobody can deny the *existence* of the messages: there they are in black and white for all the world to see. Personally I find it very difficult to visualise any explanation of the origin of these messages which does not accept discarnate communication as a fact: the alternative seems so much more difficult to believe. But if you, having read so far, think that the messages are the result of fraud or deception (conscious or otherwise) or of communication with lying or evil spirits, or of subconscious dipping into a cosmic well of untruth, or if you find any other explanation which convinces you that the messages are unworthy of careful study and attention, go your ways, friend. It is the right and duty of every human being to exercise his own brain and intelligence, and yours may be the greater wisdom—though I do not think so.

There is another book from which I have not yet quoted which deals with the tribulations of benevolent spirits who wish to help humanity.

A recently arrived spirit has had his eyes opened to human errors and misconceptions, and he breaks out into a long and impassioned speech deploring human ignorance and begging permission to return to earth and broadcast the eternal verities.

"My companion made no attempt to interrupt me, but as he walked beside me I could see a half-amused, half-regretful smile play across his face, and when I had finished, he replied in his gravely quiet tone:

NOTE

Since this book was finished I have read a book called *The Doorway* recorded by Margaret Vivian (Psychic Press, Ltd.). It is written in the simple straightforward language of an English officer, killed while saving the guns at Colenso in the Boer War. He loves horses and dogs, and has made it his work to care for stray animals in the next life. In addition to giving interesting information about the future life of animals, this book deals vividly with the puzzle of Reincarnation, which the author treats quite as a matter of course.

"There are thousands—millions of friends here who have been animated and swayed by the feelings which now move you; but when the opportunity has come and they have proceeded to carry out their noble desires, they have found that which will yet be your own experience. In the first place, you will not be believed as to your identity, and will be called upon to fight a long and by no means complimentary battle to prove you are a messenger from this life.

"Next, having gained this point in the presence of a few, they will begin to demand from you signs and wonders to strengthen this proof and gratify their curiosity. When you have succeeded in this and your heart is burning to begin your work, someone else will be brought in, and they will demand that you shall go through the unwelcome process again, for the gratification of the latecomer.

"In fact this is the normal condition in which they desire to circumscribe our work, and the greatest care is needed not to drive them away before we have attempted to sow some grain of truth.

When you reach this effort you will find that they will claim to know even more about this life than you yourself, and you must be prepared for contradiction and correction in everything you say; while many of them will generously and frequently tell you that the error you are trying to teach savours very much of the realms of darkness because it is opposed to their teachings and beliefs.

Let me advise you not to grow too enthusiastic over your anticipated mission to earth; the great majority of mankind at present prefer to postpone any definite knowledge of this life until they arrive here." (*Through the Mists*. R. J. Lees, page 18.) But whether you believe or disbelieve, beware of mockery.

Hear Zabdiel on the subject: "Did those present know that we who come to earth on our loving enterprise were angels, they would not have reviled our work of communion and those who rise above the ruck that we may make our whispers heard. No, but they do revile us and those our friends and brethren. And they shall plead their unknowing and their blindness with like effect as those who killed the Master Christ.

. . . But we do never avenge ourselves—remember you that, and remember it well. Nevertheless, in justice, and in love of our friends and co-workers in the earth plane, we do mete out punishment, and that of duty, to those who deal with them unkindly.

. . . For the rest, we do not sue on bended knee. That let them also keep in mind. We do not proffer gifts as slaves to princes.

But we do come and stand by you with gifts which gold of earth cannot buy; and to those who are humble and good and of a pure mind we give these gifts of ability to understand the Truth as it is in Jesus, of certain conviction of life beyond and of the joy of it, of fearlessness of disaster here and hereafter, and of companionship and comradeship with angels." Now I come to a great difficulty, a difficulty which I would avoid if I could. I refer to the answer which I should give to those who ask me if they should attempt to communicate from this side with the spirits of their loved ones. I say I would avoid the task if I could, because I know so little about the heart of the matter, having had, as I have already stated, no personal psychic experiences at all.

But, having undertaken to write this book, it would be unreasonable to refuse to give my own opinion on so important a subject.

My hesitation is due to the knowledge that my advice will be ignorantly bestowed, and the fear that it may be wrong. However, here goes: Throughout the messages it seems to be the newly-arrived spirits like Julia and Raymond who cry: "Communicate, communicate, communicate," while experienced spirits are more concerned to point out the difficulty of ensuring proper contact and the great danger of irresponsible and unguided "spirit-hunting." The anguish of newly-arrived spirits is not basically due to lack of power to communicate, but to the excessive and unreasonable grief of those left behind, which the spirits have no means of assuaging. The spirits, in general, want their dear ones to know, firstly, that their death should be regarded as a reason for joy and not for sorrow and, secondly, that uncontrolled grief drags them back to earth and hinders their awakening and progress.

If this view of the situation were generally accepted on earth, an infinitude of grief on both sides of the border would be obviated and the desperate urge to communicate would disappear along with the need for communication. Therefore I would say: "Do not normally attempt to initiate communication from this side, but do not repel or resist a message or an impulse to receive a communication; accept it gladly." I confidently believe that, as the years roll on, the veil between the two worlds will become thinner and thinner, and communication will become more and more a matter of course; but I think that the planning and execution of the campaign should be left to those on the other side, assisted by their specially-gifted adjutants in this life.

Now, having given that opinion with reluctance and with the greatest diffidence, here is some counsel which I offer without any diffidence at all.

Do not grieve for your dear ones, but do not forget them. Keep them always in your hearts and pray for them when they are dead just as you did when they were on earth. Your prayers can help them, and they can help you. Look forward in quiet confidence to rejoining them in God's good time; and, above all, don't expect any special signs and wonders to be worked on your behalf simply because you have adopted a new point of view towards a state of affairs which has existed from time immemorial.

And here is something else which is more than advice, it is an appeal and an injunction. If you have read this book and have been convinced of the reality of spirit-communication and of the general truth and value of the messages as a whole—don't bottle it up in your mind and keep it to yourself, but discuss it with all of your friends who are prepared to treat serious things seriously.

Here is Arnel on a case of moral cowardice. He is speaking of a man who had been taken to a rest-home in Sphere Two: "On earth he had been a minister of religion who had read somewhat of what you call psychic matters, and the possibility of speaking one to other between us and you, as we do at this present. But he could not come at the thing in thorough and was afraid to say out even so much as he in his own heart knew to be true and good So he did what many of his fellows are doing. He put the matter aside from him. He could find other ways in which to help his fellow-men, and this other matter might await the time when it was more and more widely understood and accepted of men, and then he would be one of the foremost to proclaim what he knew, and would not shirk his duty in that time.

"But when others came to him and asked him first whether it was possible to speak with their dear ones who had come over here; and second whether it were God's will so to do; he put them in mind of their Christian belief in the Saintly Communion, but urged them that they be patient until the Church should have tested and sifted and should have issued guidance for those who were of the fold.

"And while he waited, lo, his time on earth was fulfilled and he was carried over here into this Home where he might rest awhile." . . .

A messenger tells him: "The Angel who has to answer to our Master for your life-work sent me. He joys that you did good work in charity, for your heart was much bathed in love for God and man.

He sorrows for you that you were not content to do what you taught was done for you on Calvary. For you were not willing to become scorn for men, and to be withered with their disapproval, for you valued the praise of men more than God's praise, and hoped to be able one day to buy more cheaply your reward for having spread light upon the darkness when that darkness should begin to pass from night into the twilight of the dawning day. But you did not see in your weakness and lack of valiant purpose and of strength to suffer shame and coldness, that the time for which you waited would be the time when your help would not be needful, and the fight all but won by others of more stalwart mettle, while you stood with the onlookers and viewed the fight from a fair vantage-ground, while those others fought, and gave and took blows good and strong and fell forward in the battle when they would not surrender their cause to those who opposed them." If you have the leisure and the opportunity, get hold of some of these books from which I have so inadequately quoted and read them for yourself. They are much more interesting than the average novel.

Try to enlarge your horizons so that you may see this world and its happenings in their true perspective: see that what you do and try to do is most tremendously important, and that what happens to you doesn't matter at all.

Look forward to death as something infinitely to be desired when your life's work is done; and do not mourn or pity those who die before you, but think of them as fortunate. If you loved them here, keep on loving them and hold them in your heart till you meet them again.

I don't think that dogmatic Religion, in its narrow sense, matters very much. That is to say I don't think it is to be expected that we must profess a Creed in which the precise relations of Christ and God the Father are correctly defined. After all, Zabdiel, who had had a couple of centuries in heaven, said: "Little more we know, but grow in knowledge as we grow in humility and reverential love." When I was reading through this manuscript it occurred to me that "X" wasn't so far off the mark in his condensed summary for the aspirant to heaven: "The great thing is to love all the others. That is what makes them happy." But I am trespassing on the next Chapter.

CHAPTER 13

THE IMPACT OF
SPIRITUALISM ON RELIGION

As I have already stated, spiritualism is not essentially a Religion. By this I mean to say that spirit manifestations may occur, and spirit messages be received, which have nothing whatever to do with religious faith or conduct. But almost every source of spirit message transmits information, occasionally or exclusively, which is of vital importance to Religion.

Taken as a whole, the messages received over the last seventy years claim to constitute a new revelation; and, although they may not all be entirely consistent with one another, they make a combined and unanimous attack on the basic dogmas of Christian theology as at present accepted by the Protestant, Catholic and Orthodox Churches. On the other hand, they are equally unanimous in exalting the example and teaching of Jesus Christ as the one true pattern for human life and conduct.

They renew in fact the age-old struggle between the Prophet and the Priest. The Priest inevitably dislikes the Prophet, and takes every opportunity of suppressing and oppressing him, because the Prophet is continually upsetting the established order of things by new and inconvenient revelations. When a sufficient number of Prophets have been stoned, public opinion accepts their message in defiance of the Priests, and the latter are compelled to accept the new revelation and to include it in the canon of orthodoxy. Thus an uneasy equilibrium is maintained until human progress justifies a more complete revelation, and the struggle starts all over again.

The Prophets now say in effect that the Priests have had things all their own way for the last nineteen hundred years, that they have perverted the teaching of Jesus Christ so that the Christian world is sunk in a slough of materialism, and that the new revelation which they now present is long overdue.

They are sadly depressed because the world is slow to accept this new revelation. May this not be because the Prophets are now discarnate? Hitler can't cast Zabdiel into a den of lions, nor the Inquisition rack and burn Imperator. The fact is that the recipients of the messages are not always endued with the energy and the burning faith which are the attributes of the successful Prophet. The message is being imposed on their intellects, and so it is only natural that they should be objective, analytical, and careful of their name for detachment. Even the spirit Philemon remembers his earthly reputation and preserves the cloak of anonymity. True, Stead, Lodge, Vale Owen and others suffered materially for their convictions, but they were transmitters of the revelation at second or third hand instead of getting it direct from God as the Prophets of old claimed to do. The difficulty is obvious; the supply of mortals (in Western Europe at any rate) with mediumistic gifts is extremely limited, as also is the supply of souls with blazing energy and burning faith.

The combination is possibly non-existent, and so the Prophets have to rely on a rational acceptance of the written word for the success of their mission. Against them is arrayed the massed authority of the Priests, and thus the slow grinding of the Mills of God is brought almost to a standstill. Almost, but not quite! I propose to take *Spirit Teachings* as the backbone of this chapter in the same way as Vale Owen's book formed the basis for my disquisition on the afterlife.

The messages were received by the Reverend William Stainton Moses, of whose life an adequate description is given at the beginning of his book. I have no space to do more than to record a few salient facts in order to give an idea of what manner of man he was.

He was born in Lincolnshire in 1839 and his father was the headmaster of the local Grammar School. He had a brilliant school career and it was hoped that at Oxford he would take the highest honours. Unfortunately he broke down from overwork on the day before the final examination began, and he was ordered abroad for convalescence.

He spent a year on the Continent and took his degree on returning to England. He took Orders and was appointed to a curacy in the Isle of Man.

Here he distinguished himself by devoted work during a smallpox epidemic. There was no resident doctor in the district, and so great was the local panic that he had at times to combine in his own person the duties of doctor, priest and gravedigger.

The work was too arduous for his health and he moved to Douglas, I.O.M., and later to the South of England. An affliction of the throat prevented preaching or public speaking and necessitated a complete rest. This practically severed his connection with the Church.

He became a private tutor for a year and in 1870 was appointed English master in University College School where he remained for nineteen years, resigning on account of ill-health.

It was in 1870 that he first became interested in spiritualism.

At this time he had drifted into an unorthodox, almost agnostic, frame of mind and was searching for some truth more satisfying than existing doctrines. He had taken no interest in spiritualism and regarded the whole subject as "stuff and nonsense." He was convinced by visits to the mediums Lottie Fowler and Williams that some external force was at work, and his own powers began to be developed about 1872. I have already given in Chapter 3 a brief summary of the phenomena which took place under his mediumship.

He was associated with various Psychological and Spiritualistic societies, and in 1884 he founded the London Spiritualist Alliance and became its first President, a post which he held up to the time of his death in 1892.

As regards the character of Stainton Moses, his biographer stresses his individuality and force of character, his ability and versatility, and his industry and capacity for application. He had a kind and sympathetic heart and remained unspoiled by the celebrity which his gifts brought to him. "He died at his post in the prime of manhood, carrying with him to the grave the affectionate regard and esteem of hundreds who will cherish the memory of his friendship as one of their most precious legacies." The Introduction to *Spirit Teachings* was written by Stainton Moses. He explains that all the messages came by means of automatic writing, and that in almost all cases the messages, selected out of a great number for publication in his book, were originated by a spirit signing himself Imperator, but transmitted through a spirit named Rector whose control exercised the minimum of strain on the medium and whose handwriting was more legible than that of other transmitters.

The messages are not dated, but were apparently printed in the order of receipt. In selecting items for comment I have roughly followed the order of publication for ease of reference, although the messages do not appear to be arranged in any particular logical sequence such as one might perhaps expect from an instructor arranging a course of lectures. I must point out that I have merely scratched the surface of the communications as a whole, and any serious student ought to secure the book and read it all. Whether he accepts its teachings or not I can at least promise him plenty of food for thought.

Imperator endorses previous messages about the arrangement of the spheres, viz. that the three lowest spheres are nearest the earth, and that the spirits inhabiting these spheres can most easily communicate with us. Higher spirits cannot communicate unless they have what corresponds to mediumistic powers on earth. Many spirits would gladly converse, but cannot find a medium. He also issues a warning against "adversaries" or lying spirits.

The next seven spheres (up to the tenth) he calls the Spheres of Probation or Progression, and then come seven Spheres of Contemplation. He endorses the importance of the change which occurs on entering the Spheres of Contemplation, and says: "We have little from beyond, though we know that the blessed ones who dwell there have power to help and guide us even as we watch over you." And again: "We know of God, but we know Him not; nor shall know as you would seek to know, until we enter on the life of contemplation." The spheres of evil spirits are below the earth. They are minus quantities as it were; they appear to be six or eight in number.

Imperator says: "Of the lower spheres we know little." But he believes that especially obdurate spirits may so determinedly resist every good influence that they finally lose identity and become extinct. That this is the sin against the Holy Ghost, of which Jesus told His followers, and that annihilation of the soul is its reward. Remember, however, that Imperator does not teach this as a certainty, and that other spirits with greater knowledge of the lower strata tell us that every soul will eventually be saved. He endorses the general teaching that there is no personal Devil.

Imperator roundly condemns the practice of launching into spirit-life souls with angry passions stirred and vengeful feelings dominant. On these grounds he condemns both war and capital punishment as tending to increase the difficulties of mankind by the liberation of spirits with an extended capacity for mischief. He also criticises our penal system, because we shut up together numbers of evil men accompanied by their evil spirits. The result is that good spirits are drawn away and the ignorantly erring mortal is transformed into a habitual criminal. "You should teach your criminals: you should punish them, as they will be punished here, by showing them how they hurt themselves by their sin, and how they retard their future progress. You should place them where advanced and earnest spirits among you may lead them to unlearn their sin, and drink in wisdom. . . . But you horde together your dangerous spirits. You shut them up, and confine them as those beyond hope. You punish them vindictively, cruelly, foolishly: and the man who has been the victim of your ignorant treatment pursues his course of foolish, suicidal sin, until in the end you add to the list of your foolish deeds this last and worst of all, that you cut him off, debased, degraded, sensual, ignorant, mad with rage and hate, thirsting for vengeance on his fellows: you remove from him the great bar on his passions, and send him into spirit-life to work out without hindrance the devilish suggestions of his own passions.

"Blind! blind! you know not what you do. You are your own worst enemies, the truest friends of those who fight against God, and us, and you." Imperator draws a horrible picture of the spirit-neighbourhood of a gin-palace; and, in this, other spirits endorse his teaching.

They tell how besotted spirits swarm around the occupants, deriving a vicarious enjoyment from their indulgence and urging and goading them on to extremes of vicious excess. One must remember, of course, that the book was written seventy years ago and we may hope that some improvement has taken place since those days, an improvement in which economic as well as moral considerations may have played their part—gin was not 23s. a bottle in 1870.

But the general lesson is that, in all forms of vice and self-indulgence, the downward progress of the sinner is accelerated by crowds of depraved spirits who batten on the sensations of mortals, being no longer able to obtain the satisfaction which they crave from physical action of their own.

Stainton Moses attempted communication one Derby Day and could get no results. Imperator explains that on such occasions antagonistic spirits are massed together in great force to prey on those who are actuated by cupidity, drink, despair at financial loss, and immoderate excitement generally. One would have supposed that the great majority of a Derby crowd would not be obsessed by such extreme emotions, but would be bent on enjoying a cheerful holiday in the open air in convivial surroundings. That their small and unaccustomed financial flutters would have no profound spiritual effect, and that the general amateur atmosphere of the occasion would act as a protection against ill-effects. But apparently that is not the case.

At about this time Stainton Moses began to ask for proofs of the identity of the spirits who were communicating with him and showed curiosity as to the extent of their powers. Remarkable proof of identity was given in the case of one Thomas Augustine Arne, who had been communicating. Arne had been a musician, and many verifiable details of his life were given. Stainton Moses then asked if spirits could read books. The answer was that some specially qualified spirits could do so. Moses asked that one of them should be sent for. This was done.

Moses then said: "Can you go to the bookcase, take the last book but one on the second shelf and read me the last paragraph on the ninety-fourth page? I have not seen it and do not even know its name."

The spirit read: "I will curtly prove, by a short historical narrative, that property is a novelty, and has gradually arisen or grown up since the primitive and pure time of Christianity, not only since the apostolic age, but even since the lamentable union of kirk and the state by Constantine." The book proved to be a queer effusion called *Roger's Antipopopriestian* and the quotation was literally correct except that the word "narrative" had been substituted for "account." The spirit then volunteered another quotation and said: "Go and take the eleventh book on the same shelf. It will open at the page for you. Take it and read, and recognise our power, and the permission which the great and good God gives us to show you of our power over matter. To Him be Glory. Amen."

"The book (*Poetry, Romance and Rhetoric*) opened at page 145, and there was the quotation, perfectly true. I had not seen this book before: certainly had no idea of its contents." From this point onwards, more than 150 pages are devoted to the record of an interminable struggle between Stainton Moses and Imperator concerning the truth of the messages and Imperator's authority as their transmitter. Stainton Moses is supremely honest in exposing his mental processes, and it must have been difficult for him, after his eventual conviction as to the authenticity of the messages, to expose to the public gaze the tenacity with which he clung to his quite illogical standpoint, which was not the inherent value and acceptability of the messages (in which respect he was repeatedly told that he was a free agent) but the identity in earth life of Imperator as a gauge of his reliability as a communicator.

This information Imperator repeatedly and firmly refused to provide (though he gave way in a later series); but he exercised a truly angelic patience and self-control in face of Stainton Moses's obstinate adherence to his own point of view as to what Imperator ought to do to prove his bona fides. As you may have already gathered, Imperator is neither meek nor mild, and yet he exercises an iron restraint upon the intolerable irritation which even the dispassionate reader must experience in following the course of Stainton Moses's obstinacy.

I don't mean to say for a moment that Moses ought to have accepted the teaching against his own conviction as to its merits.

He was always a free agent in that respect. "But I feel that he was in a sense a representative advocate for humanity against a very stern exposition of God's love; an exposition which removes one of the stoutest props on which poor humanity has been wont to lean. I refer to the doctrine of the Redemption and Atonement. I don't think Stainton Moses put our case well for us—I will try to do it better; but first I ought to outline the revelation according to Imperator.

If Arnel and Philemon chastise orthodox theology with whips, Imperator chastises it with scorpions. Here is a sample of his numerous denunciations: "With a theology so framed, we are accused of being at variance. It is true. We have no commerce with it. It is of the earth, earthy; base and low in its conception of God; degrading in its influence on the soul; insulting to the Deity whom it professes to reveal. We have no part in it. We do indeed contradict and disown it. It is our mission to reverse its teaching, to substitute for it true and nobler views of God and of the. Spirit." The first thing which the orthodox Christian has to face is that the doctrine of the Trinity seems to have no adherents in advanced circles of the spirit world. The Divinity of Christ as a co-equal partner with tne Father is universally denied. Jesus Christ was indeed the Son of God, as also are we sons of God, for as such Christ taught us to pray to our Father. God is a universal and omnipresent Spirit, and it is foolish to take part of God's Spirit and elevate it into a Person co-equal with God.

Christ was incarnate in Jesus; but that is not the only occasion on which Christ's spirit has been manifested on earth and elsewhere.

Let Lancelot help us again: "You are wanting me to stop Mum—just one thing more then. Can you think of a Christ without Jesus? Yes, you know already Mum, how wonderful, and I thort it wouldn't be possible. It was a wonderfullest thing of all, and it was Christ Himself in another world life, and He was bringing that world to know him." These high matters are important in this life only in so far as they affect our conduct; and Imperator's chief point is that a wrong conception of God's attributes does affect our conduct on earth because we are taught to believe in the Remission of Sins to the penitent, through the virtue of Christ's sacrifice and atonement.

This doctrine Imperator vigorously combats in a score of passages throughout the book. It is difficult to select passages for quotation which do not run into hundreds of words before the subject is covered, but here are some exceptions: "Eternal justice is the correlative of eternal love. Mercy is no divine attribute. It is needless; for mercy involves remission of a penalty inflicted, and no such remission can be made save where the results have been purged away. Pity is Godlike. Mercy is human." Also: "We know nothing of the potency of blind faith and credulity. . . . We abjure and denounce that most destructive doctrine that faith, belief, assent to dogmatic statements, have power to erase the traces of transgression; that an earth lifetime of vice and sloth and sin can be wiped away and the spirit stand purified by a blind acceptance of a belief, of an idea, of a fancy, of a creed.

Such teaching has debased more souls than anything else to which we can point." And again: "Man makes his own future, stamps his own character, suffers for his own sins, and must work out his own salvation." I feel that I should have liked Stainton Moses to say, on our behalf, something on the following lines: "Dear Imperator. Thank you for the work which you are doing for our instruction and progress. Thank you for your patience with me and for the proofs which you have given of your spiritual existence and powers. I do not doubt that you are a spirit of high degree and that you are actuated by nothing but love and goodwill in your present task.

"I do not doubt that in the broad outlines of your revelation you are speaking God's truth; but be patient with me if I find it hard to accept that what we learned at our mother's knee concerning the Redemption of Sins is not true.

"We are told that it is necessary for God's inscrutable purposes that our immortal souls shall undergo a period of probation and development in mortal bodies. This principle alone makes sin inevitable. To take an extreme case, suppose that all mortals were to follow Jesus Christ's perfect example so perfectly as to refrain from marriage, God's purpose would be frustrated.

Furthermore, if the world were not a sinful place, the human soul would experience no test or struggle. Therefore sin is an essential factor in God's purpose at the present time in this world. It seems reasonable to suppose, therefore, that God would mitigate the consequences of sin to those who were penitent and believed in Him.

"Nor is this the only ground for our present beliefs. Christ said to the penitent thief on the Cross: "Today shalt thou be with Me in paradise." I do not suppose that, by that pardon, the whole of his past sins would be totally remitted without any remorse or restitution; but surely his future course would differ very materially from that of the other thief, supposing their crimes to have been approximately equal.

"Then again, there is the parable of the unmerciful servant, whose lord was moved with compassion and forgave him his debt.

It was only when the servant refused to remit a small debt due to himself that his lord was wroth and delivered him to the tormentors till he should pay all that was due unto him. I think that the saddest inscription I have ever seen on a tombstone was: 'Lord, have patience with me and I will pay thee all.' "For that matter, what did Christ mean when He taught us to pray our Father to forgive us our trespasses? "Not all angelic ministers give us identical messages and you must forgive me if I say that your message, though pure and lofty, is a little repellent in its extreme austerity.

"May we not think with Arnel, who says: 'When therefore the Ministrant . . . pleads the Sacrifice of Him who lives today very highly exalted, he in essential places his hand upon the bosom of his Lord and . . . looks towards the Father's face and pleads the love and allegiance of His Son for poor humanity's sake that they be made all as beautiful as He.' "Spiritualism ought not to be a new religion, separate, self contained, antagonistic to current Christianity; the effect of spirit communications should be to break down the barriers, not only between Christian Churches, but between Christianity and other religions. I do not suggest that you should pander to human weakness, but remember all the young people full of the throbbing blood of life. They, too, must accept the spirit message if Christ's Church Universal is to be reborn on earth." That is more or less what I should have liked Stainton Moses to say on our behalf.

Imperator's Creed is tabulated thus: Honour and love your Father God Duty to God.

(Worship).

Help your brother onward in the path
Duty to neighbour.
of progress (Brotherly love).
Tend and guard your own body.
Cultivate every means of extending knowledge.
Seek for fuller views of progressive truth.
Do ever the right and good in accordance with your knowledge.
Cultivate communion with the spirit world by prayer and frequent
intercourse.

Later on it is put somewhat differently that a man's duty to himself
is Progress, Culture and Purity. His duty to the race of which he is a
unit is Charity. And it is interesting to note that neither here nor elsewhere in the book is there any mention of that narrow aspect of Charity which consists in giving money or goods to relieve destitution. It is
taken for granted, presumably, as an act of inconsiderable merit. Even
the self-centred "X" takes the same line. In talking to a society woman,
and trying in vain to find someone with whom she has a link of love,
he asks: "Perhaps there is someone on this side whose grief you helped
to bear, whose poverty you eased?"

"I patronised our organised charities."

"I tear that sort of help is too impersonal to be remembered here."
Charity means tolerance, kindliness, unselfish helpfulness, courtesy,
honesty, sympathy, mercy, and respect for authority and for the weak.
Man's duty to God is Reverence, Adoration and Love.

There are some interesting sections on progressive revelation.

Imperator greatly exalts the spirit of Melchizedek who was the actual inspirer of Abraham. "Abraham faded from power when he passed
from the body, and in the centuries since his incarnation he has been
little concerned in influencing men.

"Melchizedek was also the inspiring spirit of Moses the lawgiver,
and Moses in his turn influenced men in many generations as the inspiring guide of Elijah." Enoch, Deborah and particularly Daniel are
mentioned as being highly gifted mediums.

The Old Testament was compiled and edited by Ezra and his scribes
out of records and legends and such other sources as were available up
to his own day. Haggai and Malachi completed the Old Testament. (In
More Spirit Teachings Imperator acknowledges his identity with Malachi.) While the Church as a whole is making up its mind about its offi-
cial attitude to Survival and Communication, may I commend this, and

other books received from spirit sources, to the attention of individual clergymen. I have already spoken of *the Scripts of Cleophas*, and there are two sequels to that book, *Paul in Athens* and *The Great Days of Ephesus*. If they had been produced as fiction by some incarnate genius they would have been hailed as masterpieces, and their value should not be diminished by the suspicion that they may be true! Imperator is particularly scathing about our marriage laws: "To the folly, and worse, to the criminal recklessness, and not less criminal and more foolish conventional law which governs the marriage customs among you, very much is chargeable. . . . You must unlearn much that men have dreamed. . . . Mistake us not! We are no advocate of licence. . . . We spurn such notions with contempt, even with more than we view the infamous buying and selling, the social slavery into which you have degraded the holiest and divinest law of life." He offers, however, no constructive suggestions.

You must realise that, contemporaneously with these messages, Stainton Moses was acting as a phenomenon-producing medium for his own "circle," and that he sometimes visited or acted for other circles during periods of disagreement with Imperator. For this latter he was reproved, but nevertheless Imperator appears to have attached a considerable value to physical manifestations as an aid to tyros or those of little faith.

It seems to me that this insistence on the importance of physical manifestations has done a good deal of harm to the Spiritualist movement in general. In the eyes of the world Spiritualists consist of groups of people sitting around rooms in the dark and deliberately deceiving themselves with childish manifestations which teach no useful lesson and lead nowhere. This may be a false judgment as regards the reality of the phenomena, but it seems reasonably sound about their value. Christ performed many miracles, presumably to indicate that One who could work such wonders would not preach to the world an empty message: but His miracles were useful and He did not do purposeless conjuring tricks. He did not yield when He was tempted: "Cast thyself down from hence." Except as a basis for scientific study with the aim of improving psychic communication, it seems to me that these manifestations do more harm than good on balance.

On one occasion Stainton Moses is rash enough to tell Imperator that he has "about as much faith as he will ever have," and incurs a lengthy and stinging rebuke in reply.

Here are a few extracts: "You are mistaken in supposing your faith to be as strong as it will be. When enlarged and purified it will be a vastly different power from that cold, calculating, nerveless assent which you now call faith. . . . Faith to be real must be outside the limits of caution and be fired by something more potent and effective than calculating prudence, or logical deduction, or judicial impartiality. It must be the fire that burns within, the mainspring that regulates the life, the over-mastering force . . . this is that which braves death and torture . . . and conducts its possessor at last to the goal.

"Of this you know nothing. Yours is not Faith, but only logical assent weighted with a mental reservation. That which you have would move no mountain, though it might suffice to select a safe way round it. . . . The time will come when you will marvel how you could have ever dig-nified this calculating caution by the name of faith. . . . When the time comes you will not set up that pale marble statue in place of what should be a living body, instinct with conviction, and energised by the loftiest purpose. You have no faith." (And that is only about half of it.) I hereby stand rebuked for my own anaemic definition of faith in Chapter 2.

To revert to what I was saying about Priests and Prophets earlier in this chapter, I suppose that the time will come when the Priest will become superfluous and will disappear. But I think that there will be need of the Priest for a long time yet.

In very early days the Priest was the Astronomer and the keeper of the Calendar, on whom men relied for knowledge concerning the time to plough their fields and sow their crops. The Astronomer Royal and the Minister of Agriculture and Fisheries now perform these functions, but the Priest remains a practical convenience for three purposes.

Firstly he should initiate the thinking on religious subjects and keep the common man up to date in progressive revelation. In this he has conspicuously failed of late years.

Secondly he should be a minister to his congregation, and help them with their problems, human and divine. In this field many priests of all denominations are earning crowns of glory.

Thirdly a priesthood is needed to organise combined worship which should be so potent a factor in our lives: and, while we have churches, there will be administrative matters which can with difficulty be han-dled by laymen.

So, although Imperator may get along very well in heaven without any priests, we shall need them here below for a good many years. But we must not sit back and think we have no responsibility for our priests. The Church is ours as well as theirs, and just as we are responsible for our Parliament, and, through it, for our Government, so we are ulti-mately responsible for our Church, our Creed, and our Priesthood.

This chapter is headed "The Impact of Spiritualism on Religion," and I shall not have touched on the heart of the matter unless I discuss its effects on the daily life of the average man and woman; and here I must say with the deepest regret that, though Spirit Teachings was written seventy years ago, though I have a reverent respect for the purity of its admonitions, and though I accord intellectual assent to almost all its teachings, even so I fear that the workaday world will not yet be able to absorb its full message and act in accordance therewith.

On the other hand I do feel that a common-sense and rational idea of what is likely to happen to normal people at death, and for a long time after death, is bound to have an improving effect on the way in which they live their present lives. The solemn thought that they will pass into the hereafter exactly the same individuals as they were on earth, and continue their lives without break or intermission in spiritual instead of earthly surroundings, must affect the outlook and conduct of all who are not wilfully blind.

The crying need of the Western world is to cut loose from its ingrained Materialism.

Most of the busy International Planners for a better post-war world are visionaries, because they are building on the postulate of an association of Christian Nations. A Christian nation is a nation of Christians, and at present there is no such thing. Maybe the Planners will give us a durable building when we give them a solid foundation for their work. Perhaps you will class me also with the Visionaries, but I prefer to think of myself as nothing worse than an Optimist.

One last word: I have made a great point in this book of my own objectivity, and my freedom from any bias due to personal psychic experience. I have therefore refrained from submitting it to any form of spiritual censorship.

But, in the process of writing the book, I have succeeded in convincing myself very definitely of the individual existence of the communicating spirits, even if I have convinced nobody else. I have tried to be honest, and I hope that lightness of touch has never degenerated into irreverence.

Here is my work for incarnate and discarnate eyes to see; and if I have erred or unwittingly misled you, I stand open to correction. And so, even as I write the words, I think that perhaps this may not really be—

THE END.

Paperbacks also available from
White Crow Books

Elsa Barker—*Letters from
a Living Dead Man*
ISBN 978-1-907355-83-7

Elsa Barker—*War Letters from
the Living Dead Man*
ISBN 978-1-907355-85-1

Elsa Barker—*Last Letters from
the Living Dead Man*
ISBN 978-1-907355-87-5

Richard Maurice Bucke—
Cosmic Consciousness
ISBN 978-1-907355-10-3

Arthur Conan Doyle—
The Edge of the Unknown
ISBN 978-1-907355-14-1

Arthur Conan Doyle—
The New Revelation
ISBN 978-1-907355-12-7

Arthur Conan Doyle—
The Vital Message
ISBN 978-1-907355-13-4

Arthur Conan Doyle with
Simon Parke—*Conversations
with Arthur Conan Doyle*
ISBN 978-1-907355-80-6

Meister Eckhart with Simon Parke—
Conversations with Meister Eckhart
ISBN 978-1-907355-18-9

D. D. Home—*Incidents in my Life Part 1*
ISBN 978-1-907355-15-8

Mme. Dunglas Home; edited,
with an Introduction, by Sir
Arthur Conan Doyle—*D. D.
Home: His Life and Mission*
ISBN 978-1-907355-16-5

Edward C. Randall—
Frontiers of the Afterlife
ISBN 978-1-907355-30-1

Rebecca Ruter Springer—
Intra Muros: My Dream of Heaven
ISBN 978-1-907355-11-0

Leo Tolstoy, edited by Simon
Parke—*Forbidden Words*
ISBN 978-1-907355-00-4

Leo Tolstoy—*A Confession*
ISBN 978-1-907355-24-0

Leo Tolstoy—*The Gospel in Brief*
ISBN 978-1-907355-22-6

Leo Tolstoy—*The Kingdom
of God is Within You*
ISBN 978-1-907355-27-1

Leo Tolstoy—*My Religion:
What I Believe*
ISBN 978-1-907355-23-3

Leo Tolstoy—*On Life*
ISBN 978-1-907355-91-2

Leo Tolstoy—*Twenty-three Tales*
ISBN 978-1-907355-29-5

Leo Tolstoy—*What is Religion
and other writings*
ISBN 978-1-907355-28-8

Leo Tolstoy—*Work While
Ye Have the Light*
ISBN 978-1-907355-26-4

Leo Tolstoy—*The Death of Ivan Ilyich*
ISBN 978-1-907661-10-5

Leo Tolstoy—*Resurrection*
ISBN 978-1-907661-09-9

Leo Tolstoy with Simon Parke—
Conversations with Tolstoy
ISBN 978-1-907355-25-7

Howard Williams with an Introduction
by Leo Tolstoy—*The Ethics of Diet:
An Anthology of Vegetarian Thought*
ISBN 978-1-907355-21-9

Vincent Van Gogh with Simon
Parke—*Conversations with Van Gogh*
ISBN 978-1-907355-95-0

Wolfgang Amadeus Mozart with Simon
Parke—*Conversations with Mozart*
ISBN 978-1-907661-38-9

Jesus of Nazareth with Simon Parke—
Conversations with Jesus of Nazareth
ISBN 978-1-907661-41-9

Thomas à Kempis with Simon
Parke—*The Imitation of Christ*
ISBN 978-1-907661-58-7

Julian of Norwich with Simon
Parke—*Revelations of Divine Love*
ISBN 978-1-907661-88-4

Allan Kardec—*The Spirits Book*
ISBN 978-1-907355-98-1

Allan Kardec—*The Book on Mediums*
ISBN 978-1-907661-75-4

Emanuel Swedenborg—*Heaven and Hell*
ISBN 978-1-907661-55-6

P.D. Ouspensky—*Tertium Organum:
The Third Canon of Thought*
ISBN 978-1-907661-47-1

Dwight Goddard—*A Buddhist Bible*
ISBN 978-1-907661-44-0

Michael Tymn—*The Afterlife Revealed*
ISBN 978-1-970661-90-7

Michael Tymn—*Transcending the
Titanic: Beyond Death's Door*
ISBN 978-1-908733-02-3

Guy L. Playfair—*If This Be Magic*
ISBN 978-1-907661-84-6

Guy L. Playfair—*The Flying Cow*
ISBN 978-1-907661-94-5

Guy L. Playfair —*This House is Haunted*
ISBN 978-1-907661-78-5

Carl Wickland, M.D.—
Thirty Years Among the Dead
ISBN 978-1-907661-72-3

John E. Mack—*Passport to the Cosmos*
ISBN 978-1-907661-81-5

Peter & Elizabeth Fenwick—
The Truth in the Light
ISBN 978-1-908733-08-5

Erlendur Haraldsson—
Modern Miracles
ISBN 978-1-908733-25-2

Erlendur Haraldsson—
At the Hour of Death
ISBN 978-1-908733-27-6

Erlendur Haraldsson—
The Departed Among the Living
ISBN 978-1-908733-29-0

Brian Inglis—*Science and Parascience*
ISBN 978-1-908733-18-4

Brian Inglis—*Natural and Supernatural:
A History of the Paranormal*
ISBN 978-1-908733-20-7

Ernest Holmes—*The Science of Mind*
ISBN 978-1-908733-10-8

Victor & Wendy Zammit —*A Lawyer
Presents the Evidence For the Afterlife*
ISBN 978-1-908733-22-1

Casper S. Yost—*Patience
Worth: A Psychic Mystery*
ISBN 978-1-908733-06-1

William Usborne Moore—
Glimpses of the Next State
ISBN 978-1-907661-01-3

William Usborne Moore—
The Voices
ISBN 978-1-908733-04-7

John W. White—
The Highest State of Consciousness
ISBN 978-1-908733-31-3

Stafford Betty—
The Imprisoned Splendor
ISBN 978-1-907661-98-3

Paul Pearsall, Ph.D. —
Super Joy
ISBN 978-1-908733-16-0

**All titles available as eBooks, and selected titles available in Hardback and
Audiobook formats from www.whitecrowbooks.com**

Printed in November 2021
by Rotomail Italia S.p.A., Vignate (MI) - Italy